Talking to Parents

Edited by

CLARE WINNICOTT

CHRISTOPHER BOLLAS

MADELEINE DAVIS

RAY SHEPHERD

Talking to Parents

D.W. WINNICOTT

Introduction by
T. BERRY BRAZELTON, M.D.

A Merloyd Lawrence Book

Addison-Wesley Publishing Company

Reading, Massachusetts   Menlo Park, California   New York
Don Mills, Ontario   Wokingham, England   Amsterdam
Bonn   Sydney   Singapore   Tokyo   Madrid
San Juan   Paris   Seoul   Milan   Mexico City   Taipei

Library of Congress Cataloging-in-Publication Data

Winnicott, D. W. (Donald Woods), 1896–1971.
 Talking to parents / D. W. Winnicott ; introduction by T. Berry Brazelton ; edited by Clare Winnicott, Christopher Bollas, Madeleine Davis, Ray Shepherd.
  p. cm.
 "A Merloyd Lawrence book."
 Includes bibliographical references and index.
 ISBN 0-201-60893-6
 1. Parenting—United States. 2. Child rearing—United States.
 3. Parent and child—United States. I. Winnicott, Clare.
 II. Title.
 HQ755.8.W6 1993
 306.874—dc20   92-36863
                                                    CIP

Chapters 7 and 10 are reprinted from *The Family and Individual Development* (1965) by D. W. Winnicott, with the kind permission of Tavistock Publications.

Jacket design by Diana Coe
Text design by Janis Owens
Set in 11-point Caslon 540 by Compset, Inc.

1 2 3 4 5 6 7 8 9-MU-9796959493
First printing, February 1993

Acknowledgment

Madeleine Davis died while working on the last stages of preparation for this book. Sadly, she has not lived to see its publication but the publishers, the editors, and all those involved with The Winnicott Trust wish to record their admiration and gratitude for her gracious and thoughtful help in preparing this and previous Winnicott works for publication.

The editors would like to thank Tavistock Publications for permission to include previously published material. Thanks are also due to the BBC, without whose foresight many of the talks on which this book is based may not have taken place, and to Claire Rayner for her thoughtful contribution to chapter 8.

Contents

On Reading Winnicott
T. BERRY BRAZELTON, M.D.   ix

Editors' Preface   xiii

ONE
Health Education through Broadcasting   1

TWO
For Stepparents   7

THREE
What Do We Know about Babies as Cloth Suckers?   15

FOUR
Saying "No"   21

FIVE
Jealousy   41

SIX
What Irks?   65

SEVEN
Security   87

EIGHT
Feeling Guilty   95

NINE
The Development of a Child's Sense of Right and Wrong   105

TEN
Now They Are Five   111

ELEVEN
The Building Up of Trust   121

Original Source of Each Chapter   135
Bibliographical Note: The Works of D. W. Winnicott   137
Index   139
About the Author   143

On Reading Winnicott

T. BERRY BRAZELTON, M.D.

Reading these largely unpublished pieces by D. W. Winnicott is like returning to a refreshing spring after a walk in the desert. Each one is an utterly rewarding, delightful experience.

The very fact that Winnicott chose to address parents directly through the media is of great interest. After all, his ideal "ordinary devoted mother" is one who practices her child care unself-consciously. This broadcasting of his child-rearing ideas could be seen as flaunting his own philosophy. But, as is his wont, he immediately lays one's question to rest. He is not trying to instruct parents but to help them understand what they do and then to justify them for what they have done. A statement such as "One can only see that one might have done the same, or one might have done worse" illustrates his simple but powerful way of backing up parents for their strengths, unlike the usual parenting authority who so expertly tells parents what not to do.

I have been an admirer and a student of Donald Winnicott all my professional life. The way he combined a normative pediatric approach with the insights of child psychiatry and psychoanalysis made him my model long ago. His own brilliant insights are based on a deep understanding of the parent-infant processes coupled with firm conviction that most parents want desperately to do well by their children. These essays are sprinkled with his positively reinforcing interpretations. Parents will feel liberated and reassured by them, for they are delivered right from the heart, and with his deliciously quirky wit.

As he makes clear, the purpose of these talks was not to tell parents what to do, but (1) to detoxify the science of child-rearing, (2) to give them confidence in what they were doing, and (3) to free them to seek individualized help when they hit a snag in parenting their children. He continually emphasizes the parent's instinct to do the right thing, coupled with the inevitable guilt and ambivalence that makes them the sensitive parents that they are. He is never afraid of honest common sense: "A meeting of unsuccessful stepparents... might be fruitful. It would be composed of ordinary men and women." For being a stepparent is an unavoidably unrewarding role.

In the essay on thumb-sucking, he gives the best justification I have heard. Sucking on the thumb is the baby's first use of imagination. The real experience of sucking on his thumb has been enriched by the imagined breast or bottle. Why would anyone deprive him of this first experience in creating his own affectionate object?

These talks pare down to their essence the simple steps that lead to the parenting goals he is discussing. For example, the three stages of saying "No" start with the parents' need to assume full responsibility for the child's limits (first year), teaching him the word "no" and words associated with danger, such as "hot" (second year), and then, turning it back to him and enlarging on his choice-making experience and his ability to incorporate these limits, giving him verbal explanations (third year).

Take another question dear to the hearts of parents: "How does jealousy disappear?" In Winnicott's beautifully spare explanation we see how it is eventually defused by identifying with the person of whom one is so jealous, then by identifying with the jealously guarding mother and her feelings, using one's imagination (empathy) to take the other's perspective.

I think my favorite is the piece on "what's irksome" about being a parent. This chapter will help all parents face their negative feelings as normal and even healthy. Winnicott reminds us that what goes wrong is always irksome; when it goes right it gets ignored. So, of course, the parents' day becomes loaded with the irksome details of day-to-day living. "Children will go on being a nuisance and mothers will go on being glad they had the chance to be the victims."

This is a beautiful little volume. Winnicott distills the essential nature of being a parent. For instance, chapter 8 concludes with the provocative idea that, without guilt and ambivalence, no mother would be sensitive to her child's needs. He indeed infuses the reader with an understanding of the challenges of parenting, but he also makes his audience feel that being a "good enough mother" is one of the most gratifying roles one could seek. What a genius!

Editors' Preface

Between 1939 and 1962 Donald Winnicott gave about fifty radio talks for the BBC, nearly all of them to parents. Transcribed, they turn out to contain some of his most lucid and compelling writing. A collection of the earlier talks, broadcast towards the end of the war, with Janet Quigley as producer, gave rise to a pamphlet entitled *Getting to Know Your Baby*. Another series, dating from 1949 to 1950, under the production of Isa Benzie, was published in a similar pamphlet called *The Ordinary Devoted Mother and Her Baby*. Both went fairly quickly out of print. Though Winnicott, because of the rules prohibiting doctors from advertising, had not put his name to the broadcasts, a following grew up, and there were many requests that the talks be reissued. It thus came about that these formed the basis of a book entitled *The Child and the Family*, edited by Janet Hardenberg and issued by Tavistock Publications in 1957*; a few more talks, mainly about wartime evacuation, were included in its companion volume, *The Child and the Outside World*. In 1964 Penguin Books decided to publish a selection from these two volumes under the title *The Child, the Family, and*

*Published in the United States by Basic Books under the title *Mother and Baby: A Primer in First Relationships*.

xiv ☘ TALKING TO PARENTS

the Outside World, which included nearly all of the broadcast talks published up to that time.

By the end of 1968, 50,000 copies of the Penguin edition had been sold, and Winnicott wrote a short speech for a party given in celebration. In it he tells of how, for some of the earlier talks, he would go to the BBC in Langham Place "driving his car over the glass and rubble of the previous night's air-raid." He goes on to say how much he was helped in the long series of talks in 1949–50 by Isa Benzie, who transmitted her enthusiasm for and confidence in his work to him and, in his words, "pulled the phrase 'the ordinary devoted mother' out of what I had talked about." He continues: "This immediately became a peg to hang things on, and it suited my need to get away from both idealisation and also from teaching and propaganda. I could get on with a description of child care as practised unselfconsciously everywhere."

Interestingly, Winnicott also makes the point that after the war he did not resume the practice of paediatrics (though he still held psychiatric clinics for children) and consequently was not so closely in touch as he had previously been with a mass of everyday material relating to mother-child interaction. For these talks he therefore found it necessary to "rekindle the clinical flame" by using material from "the regressive experiences of psycho-analytic patients, many of them adult, who were giving me a close-up of the mother-infant (or parent-infant) relationship." "At the time of these BBC broadcasts in the late forties," he wrote, "I was in a unique position, being able to see my patients in terms of both paediatrics and of a kind of psychoanalysis that was peculiarly my own. Naturally in talking over the radio I needed to keep to the language of paediatrics, though it can be seen that paediatrics for me had already become a place for the study of the infant-mother emotional tie, assuming (as one usually can do) physical health. I had moved from 'infant feeding' to 'the infant-mother mutual involvement.'"

Winnicott's book *The Child, the Family, and the Outside World* has retained its popularity up to today and still sells thousands of copies a year. It has recently been republished in the United States by Addison-Wesley.

The present volume, *Talking to Parents*, gathers together all the broadcast talks that were given after 1955. Only two of these have been published before: "Now They Are Five" (under the title "The Five-Year-Old") and "Security" (under the title "On Security") in Winnicott's book *The Family and Individual Development*.* We have included them for the sake of completeness. Also included are two papers not written for broadcasting: "Health Education through Broadcasting" is used as an introductory chapter because it states so clearly the aims that Winnicott came to see as important in giving radio talks; we have added "The Building up of Trust" because it was written for parents (something rare for Winnicott outside broadcasting), has not yet been published, and, dating as it does from his last years, contains many of his essential ideas about children and their parents that he had spent his professional life developing. We have not been able to discover the exact audience for whom it was composed.

---

*London: Tavistock, 1965; New York: Basic Books, 1965.

The collating and editing of the papers were nearly completed with the help of Clare Winnicott before her death in 1984. The editing has been kept to a minimum: hardly any editing of the radio talks themselves was necessary, as they appear to have been written by Winnicott before being broadcast; they were found in typescript among many other papers left by him. The exceptions are the two talks to stepmothers and the discussion with Claire Rayner about "Feeling Guilty." These have been transcribed from tapes, and the quality of the writing is therefore not quite the same. This also applies to the conversations between mothers that appear as part of the central series of talks ("Saying 'No'," "Jealousy," and "What Irks?"). For these the mothers were invited to the BBC, their conversations were recorded, and Winnicott made his comments on them on a different day; but here the unrehearsed nature of what was said becomes an essential ingredient of the whole.

Christopher Bollas
Madeleine Davis
Ray Shepherd

LONDON, 1992

ONE

Health Education
through Broadcasting

This article is written by invitation. The subject of
health education through broadcasting is one that has interest for me since I have from time to time given talks over
the air to parents. But it should be made clear that I am not
in fact especially in favour of health education in mass
form. When an audience is vast it contains many people
who are not listening for the purpose of learning, but who
are listening by chance or for fun, or perhaps even while
they are shaving or making cakes, and so have no free hand
to turn the knob. In such conditions one must surely have
grave doubts as to the value of putting across anything that
is important.

One may compare this with school broadcasting, where
children of known ages are sitting around, suitably occu-
pied in a mild way, but definitely expecting that for a period
of time they will be receiving instruction given in an interesting way from the radio. The broadcaster who wishes to
talk about health has not the advantage of a special audience.

I am referring to health education in terms of psychology
and not to education in matters of physical health and in
the prevention and treatment of diseases. Much of what I

have to say, however, could be applied to any talks on health, because it seems to me that all health education is psychological. Those who listen to a talk on rheumatism or on blood diseases do not do so because they have a scientific interest in the subject, or because of a hunger for facts; they do it because they are morbidly interested in disease. It seems to me that in educating people in matters of health this applies, whatever the medium used, except for the complication that in broadcasting one must expect that the vast majority of people who are listening in are not interested in being taught anything at all and are merely waiting for music to restart. Perhaps I am maligning the listener, but I am at any rate expressing a doubt that I feel every time the optimistic and reassuring voice of the health doctor gives a heartening talk on the Rhesus factor, or rheumatoid arthritis, or cancer.

I do wish to make one constructive suggestion, however, with reference to broadcasting in health matters. Any kind of propaganda, or telling people what to do, is to be deplored. It is an insult to indoctrinate people, even for their own good, unless they have the chance by being present to react, to express disapproval, and to contribute.

Is there an alternative that we may allow? What one can do as an alternative is to attempt to get hold of the ordinary things that people do, and to help them to understand why they do them. The basis for this suggestion is the idea that much that people do is really sensible in the circumstances. It is astonishing how, when one listens over and over again to the descriptions mothers give of the management of a child in the home, in the end one comes down to feeling that one cannot tell these parents what to do; one can only see that one might have done the same, or one might have done worse in the circumstances.

What people do like is to be given an understanding of the problems that they are tackling, and they like to be made aware of the things that they do intuitively. They feel unsafe when left to their hunches, to the sort of things that come to them at the critical moment, when they are not thinking things out. It may be that parents gave a child a smack or a kiss or a hug or they laughed. Something appropriate happened. This was the right thing, nothing could have been better. No-one could have told these parents what to do in the circumstances, because the circumstances could not have been described in advance. Afterwards, however, the parents find themselves talking things over and wondering, and often they have no notion what they have been doing and they feel confused about the problem itself. At such a moment they tend to feel guilty, and they fly to anyone who will speak with authority, who will give orders.

Education can catch on to all these things that people do and indeed have done, and in a good way, ever since the world started to have human beings in it who were human. If one can really show people what they are doing they become less frightened, they feel more secure about themselves, so that when they are genuinely in doubt or genuinely know that they are ignorant they seek not advice but information. The reason why they seek information is that they begin to have an idea where to go for it. They begin to see that it is possible to adopt an objective approach towards matters of the mind and of feeling and of behaviour, and they become less suspicious of science, even when it encroaches on those areas which till recently have been the exclusive property of religion.

I would think that there is a very great deal to be done in this matter of taking what people feel and think and do and building upon this foundation discussion or teaching which makes for a better understanding. In this way information can be passed on without there being an undermining of the self-confidence of the listener. The difficulty is for those who do the teaching in this way to know enough and to know when they themselves are ignorant.

Sometimes a broadcast talk to parents implies: "You ought to love your child; if you don't love your child the child will suffer, will become a delinquent." "You must breast-feed your infant; you must enjoy breast-feeding your infant; this must be the most important thing in your life." "You must love your baby as soon as the baby is born; it's unnatural not to love your own baby"... and so on and so on. All these things are very easy to say but in fact if said they produce deplorable effects.

It would be helpful to point out to mothers that sometimes mothers do not love their babies at first, or to show why mothers often find themselves unable to feed the baby at the breast, or to explain why loving is a complex matter, and not just an instinct.

I would like to add this, that it is not possible, in talking over the wireless, to deal with gross abnormalities, either in the mother or in the child, especially abnormalities in the parents. There is no point in telling people who have difficulties that they are ill. When ill people apply for help we must take the opportunity to relieve them where we can, but we easily cause distress if we make people feel ill without being available with therapy.

Almost every bit of advice that one gives over the air gives distress somewhere. Recently I spoke about telling adopted children that they are adopted. I knew of course that I was in danger of causing distress. No doubt I did upset many, but one mother who had listened came to me from a long way away and told me exactly why it would be very dangerous *in the circumstances* to tell her adopted child that she was adopted. I had to agree, although in principle I know that it is right to tell adopted children that they are adopted, and to do so as soon as possible.

If mothers are told to do this or that or the other, they soon get into a muddle, and (what is most important of all) they lose touch with their own ability to act without knowing exactly what is right and what is wrong. Only too easily they feel incompetent. If they must look up everything in a book or listen on the wireless, they are always too late even when they do the right things, because the right things have to be done immediately. It is only possible to act at exactly the right point when the action is intuitive or by instinct, as we say. The mind can be brought to bear on the problem afterwards, and when people think things out our job is to help them. We may discuss with them the sort of problems that they are faced with, and the sort of things they do, and the sort of effect that they may expect from their actions. This need not be the same as telling them what to do.

Finally: is there a place for formal instruction over the air in child psychology? It is doubtful to me whether we are ready to give instruction of this kind. Also I am reminded of the fact that in giving instruction to groups of students (social workers, for instance, or post-graduate teachers, or doctors), one knows that such instruction cannot be given loosely, but must be given within a formal setting. Perhaps over a period of time these students are having instruction; they are given opportunity for discussing among themselves what they are told, and for reading, and they have opportunity for expressing disagreement and for contributing. Even in these favourable circumstances a proportion of those who are receiving instruction will have personal difficulties to contend with, personal difficulties brought out by the new ideas and the new approach and by the revival of difficult memories and repressed fantasies. They will have had to deal with new excitements and with a rearrangement of their philosophy of life. Instruction in psychology is not like instruction in physics or even in biology.

Instruction of parents could be done, no doubt, in a carefully controlled situation, but instruction given over the wireless is not in this category. If given it must be of an extremely restricted variety, catching up on the good things that happen to normal people. Along these lines, however, a great deal can be done, and it is to be hoped that it will remain the policy of the BBC to render social service by giving time for health education that takes into account the difficulties inherent in broadcasting.

[1957]

TWO

For Stepparents

The Wicked Stepmother

The suggestion is sometimes made that were it not for fairy stories, ideas like that of the wicked stepmother wouldn't arise at all. I myself am sure this is wrong and that it is more true to say that no fairy story, or horror comic for that matter, can have universal appeal unless it deals with something that is inherent in each individual adult or child. What the fairy story does is to catch on to something that is true, frightening and unacceptable. Yes, all three; true, frightening and unacceptable. Little bits of the unacceptable in human nature crystallize out into the accepted myth. The question is, what crystallizes out into the step-mother myth? Whatever it is, it has to do with hate and fear as well as with love.

Each individual has a great difficulty in gathering to-gether the aggressiveness that there is in human nature and mixing it with loving. To some extent this difficulty is over-come in earliest infancy by the fact that at first the world is felt in extremes, friendly and hostile, good and hostile, black and white; the bad is feared and hated and the good is wholly accepted. Gradually infants and children grow up

7

out of this and reach the stage where they can tolerate having destructive ideas along with their loving impulses. They then feel guilt but they find they can do things to make good. If mother will wait the moment will come for the gesture of love that is genuine and spontaneous. The relief normally afforded in the earliest stages by the idea of the good and bad extremes is something that even mature adults cannot altogether forego. Children, and little children in particular, we easily allow some persistence of this relic of infancy, and we know we can find a ready response when we read or tell stories which present the good and bad extremes.

Usually the real mother and the stepmother join up in the imagination with these extremes, and especially so because of the second thing that I want to describe which is that there are all sorts of reasons why children could hate their mothers. This idea of a hate of a mother is very difficult for everyone and some who are listening will not like to hear the word hate and mother put in the same sentence. However, it can't be helped; mothers, if they do their job properly, are the representatives of the hard, demanding world and it is they who gradually introduce reality which is so often the enemy of impulse. There is anger with mother and hatred is somewhere even when there is absolutely no doubt of love that is mixed with adoration. If there are two mothers, a real one who has died, and a stepmother, do you see how easily a child gets relief from tension by having one perfect and the other horrid? This is almost as true of the world's expectations as of a child's beliefs.

On top of all this a child comes to see or to feel eventually that mother's devotion at a very early stage has provided the essential conditions that enabled him or her to start, to start to exist as a person, with personal rights, personal impulses and a personal technique of living. In other words, there was absolute dependence in the beginning and as the child begins to be able to realize this so there develops a fear of a primeval mother who has magic powers for good and evil. How difficult it is for each one of us to see that this all-powerful primeval agency was our own mother, someone we have come to know as a lovable, but not by any means perfect or perfectly reliable, human being. How precarious it all was. And further, in the case of a girl, it is this same mother, who was at first all-powerful, who maddeningly represented hard fact, who was all the time adorable, who actually comes to stand in between the daughter and the father. Here in particular, the real mother and the stepmother start from different places; for the real mother hopes while the stepmother fears that the girl will win her father's love. Isn't this enough to show that we must not expect children to grow up all of a sudden from a tendency to split up the world in general and their two mothers in particular into good and bad, and that we must expect some persistence of these childhood ideas in adults?

We can use logical argument, we can tell ourselves over and over again that what matters is not whether people are black or white but whether they as human beings are loving and lovable. But we are left with our dreams and who would wish to be rid of fantasies? In fantasy we don't need to be grown up all the time in the way we need to be when we catch the train to the office or when we do the shopping. In fantasy the infantile, the childish and the adolescent all lie down with adult maturity. But we notice the inconvenience of fantasy when we happen to split into one or other of the black characteristics of the world's myths. I myself may have slipped into one perhaps by talking about the hate and the fear of mother that I feel has to be mixed in with the love in the fully experienced child-mother relationships. You may think I'm nuts.

The Value of the Unsuccess Story

In the study of any problem to do with human affairs we can keep superficial or we can go deep. If we could keep superficial we avoid a lot of unpleasantness but we also avoid deeper values. Some of the letters that came in after the recent broadcast did go beyond the obvious. For instance it was pointed out that the child who has lost the parent cannot be treated as if this had not happened and often it is preferable for a stepmother or a stepfather to allow another name so that the child keeps the name Mummy or Daddy for the parent lost. The idea of the lost parent can be kept alive and the child can be greatly helped by the attitude which makes this possible. Also it was pointed out that the child taken over may be disturbed; and in this special case of a child who was not loved, the boy had had a period with the grandmother before coming to the stepmother so that he was twice deprived and consequently liable to feel hopeless about human relationships and dependabilities. If a child feels hopeless in this way then he cannot take the risk of starting up new ties and defends himself against feeling deeply and against new dependencies.

Do you know that quite a lot of mothers do not love their own infants at the time they give birth to them? They feel awful, just like the stepmother. They try to pretend they love but they just can't. How much easier for them if they had been told in advance that love is a thing that may come but it cannot be turned on. Usually a mother soon comes to love, to love her infant during her pregnancy, but this is a matter for experience, not for conventional expectation. Fathers have the same problem sometimes. Perhaps this is more easily accepted, so there is less need for fathers to pretend and their love can come naturally and in its own time. Apart from not loving, mothers not infrequently hate their babies. I am speaking of ordinary women who in fact manage quite well and who see to it that someone acts for them and acts well. I know of many mothers who lived in dread lest they should find that they have harmed their own infants and they can never talk of their difficulty because of it being so unlikely that they could get understanding. There is so much in human nature that is deep and hidden and personally I would rather be the child of a mother who has all the inner conflicts of the human being than be mothered by someone for whom all is easy and smooth, who knows all the answers, and is a stranger to doubt.

Most of those who claimed success here and there could register unsuccess somewhere else, and in the right place and in the right time the unsuccess story has the very greatest value. Of course it is another matter when people go around moaning and groaning but this is certainly not what happened with our stepmother who suffered so much because she could not love her stepson. Whenever a wife or a husband takes over a stepchild there is always a lot of back history, and this back history makes all the difference. It is not just a matter of guilt feeling because of a child that is, so to speak, stolen; there is a whole story of a choice of a widow or widower, or the rescue of a person unhappily married. There are a whole host of important issues that cannot be ignored and which affect the stepparent's dream or imaginative background to the new relationship. In any one case things can be examined, and even usefully examined, but in talking generally the subject immediately becomes too vast to be covered. The woman who finds herself mothering a child who was born of a woman who is imaginatively her rival, even if dead, may easily find herself forced by her own imagination into the position of witch rather than of fairy godmother. She may indeed find no difficulty or she may, as some of the letter-writers described, like to take second place to the former wife. But many men and women are still struggling to grow up when they marry and after, and they must fight for their own rights or lose their identity and their whole feeling of being real. A woman may easily feel the presence of the other woman's child to be a reminder of the child's mother and an intolerable reminder. If this sort of thing is true and yet unconscious it can distort the picture and make impossible a natural growth of feelings towards tolerance and then love.

I have only time to mention the fact that a proportion of stepchildren are really nasty on account of the experiences they have been through. One can explain them and excuse them but the stepmother has to endure them. There is no way out for her. Fortunately most stepchildren are able to be brought round to a friendly attitude and indeed, as the letters show, in very many cases the stepchildren are just exactly like the mother's own. So often there are no difficulties or the difficulties are not big and present no threat. Many people lose sight of the perplexity of the step-situation and come to believe it is all quite simple. For people with no difficulties my sort of probing into the imaginative world must seem irksome, even dangerous. It is dangerous to their sense of security but as I have said, by losing sight of the bad dreams and even nightmares and of the depressions and suspicions that they came through they also lose sight of all that which makes sense of their achievement.

A smattering of unsuccess stories can greatly enrich our lives. Moreover, these stories can show us that there is a point in helping unsuccessful people to get together. If they get together and talk they share their burdens and sometimes lighten them. A correspondent asked for a meeting of unsuccessful stepparents. I think such a meeting might be fruitful. It would be composed of ordinary men and women.

[1955]

THREE

What Do We Know about Babies as Cloth Suckers?

There's a great deal to be got out of watching what babies do in passing the time between sleeps. But first we must get free from the idea that there is a right and a wrong; our interest arises out of the fact that from babies we can learn about babies. The speaker last week took the point of view that if a particular infant sucks his thumb or a cloth that's not where we come in to approve or to disapprove, but it's where we have a chance to get to know something about that particular infant. I agree with him and with the mothers from whose letters he quoted.

We are concerned with a wide variety of phenomena that characterise infant life. We can never know all about these because there's always a new infant, and no two infants are exactly alike either in face or in habits. We know babies not only by the line of their nose and the colour of their hair, if any, but also by their idiosyncrasies.

When mothers tell me about children I usually get them to remember what sort of things happened at the very beginning which were characteristic. They rather like reminding themselves of these things which bring up the past so vividly.

They tell me about all sorts of objects which become adopted by the infant, and which become important, and get sucked or hugged, and which tide the infant over moments of loneliness and insecurity, or provide solace, or which act as a sedative. The objects are halfway between being part of the infant and part of the world. Soon they are apt to acquire a name, like "tissie" or "nammie," which betrays their double origin. Their smell and texture are their essential elements, and you dare not wash them. Nor do you leave such an object behind when going away from home. If you are wise you let the object fade away, like the old soldier of the song who never dies; you don't destroy it or lose it or give it away.

The main thing is that you never challenge the infant: "Is this thing something you thought up, or is it part of the world that you found and took to yourself?" A little later and you will be enjoining your infant to say "ta," and so to acknowledge that that woolly dog came as a present from an aunt. But this *first* object is established as part of the furniture of the cot and pram before the word "ta" can be said or could make sense, before the infant makes a clear distinction between the me and the not-me, or while the making of this distinction is in process.

A personality is being formed and a life is being lived that has never been lived before, and this new person living this new life is what the mother and father are interested in from the moment the infant is felt to be moving in the womb. The personal life starts right away, and I shall stick to this idea even although I know that puppies and kittens also suck cloths and play, a fact which makes me say that animals, too, are more than just bundles of reflexes and appetites.

When I say that life starts right away I admit that at first life takes a very restricted form, but the personal life of the infant has certainly started by the time of birth. These odd habits of infants tell us that there is something more in infant life than sleeping and getting milk, and something more than getting instinctual gratification from a good feed taken in and kept down. These habits indicate that an infant is there already, actually living a life, building up memories, forming a personal pattern of behaviour.

To understand further I think we must reckon that there is in being from the first a crude form of what later we call the imagination. This enables us to say that the infant takes in with the hands and with the sensitive skin of the face as well as with the mouth. The *imaginative* feeding experience is much wider than the purely physical experience. The *total* experience of feeding can quickly involve a rich relationship to the mother's breast, or to the mother as gradually perceived, and what the baby does with the hands and eyes widens the scope of the feeding act. This which is normal is made more plain when we see an infant's feed being managed in a mechanical way. Such a feed, far from being an enriching experience for the infant, interrupts the infant's sense of going on being. I don't know quite how else to put it. There has been a reflex activity and no personal experience.

When you tickle an infant's face you can produce a smile, but the infant may be feeling anything but pleased. The reflex has betrayed its owner. It almost owns the infant. It is not our job to wield the power we undoubtedly possess by eliciting reflexes, and by stimulating instinctual gratifications that do not arise as part of the rhythm of the infant's personal life.

All sorts of things an infant does while feeding seem senseless to us because they don't put on weight. I am saying that it is just these very things that reassure us that the infant is feeding, not just *being fed*, is living a life and not just responding to the stimuli we offer.

Have you ever seen an infant sucking a finger at the same time as happily breast-feeding? I have. Have you ever seen a dream walking? When an infant sucks bits of clothing, or the eiderdown or a dummy, this represents a spillover of the imagination, such as it is, imagination stimulated by the central exciting function which is feeding.

I will put it another way. Have you ever thought that the feeling round and the finger-sucking and the sucking of cloths and the clutching of the rag doll is the infant's first show of affectionate behaviour? Can anything be more important?

You perhaps take your infant's capacity for being affectionate for granted, but you soon know about it if you have a child that cannot show affection or who has lost the art. It may be possible to induce a child to eat who seems unwilling, but there is nothing you can do to make an unaffectionate child affectionate. You can shower affection on him but he turns away, either silently or with screams of protest.

These odd, off-the-mark activities that we are talking about are a sign that the infant is there as a person and, moreover, confident in the relationship to the mother. The infant is able to use objects that are symbolic, as we would say, of the mother or of some quality of the mother, and is able to *enjoy* actions that are only *playing*, and are at one or more removed from the *instinctual* act, that is to say, *feeding*.

Look at what happens if the infant begins to lose confidence. A minor deprivation may produce a compulsive element in the sucking habit, or whatever it is, so that it becomes a main line instead of a branch line. But if there should be a more severe or prolonged deprivation the infant loses all the capacity to suck the bit of cloth or to play with his mouth or to tickle his nose; the meaning goes out of these play activities.

These first play objects and these play activities exist in a world between the infant and the external world. There's a tremendous strain behind the infant's delay in distinguishing between the me and the not-me, and we allow time for this development to take place naturally. We see the infant beginning to sort things out and to know that there is a world outside and a world within, and in order to help we allow an intermediate world, one which is at the same time both personal and external, both me and not-me. This is the same as the intense play of early childhood and the day-dreaming of older children or adults, which is neither dream nor fact, yet it is both.

Come to think of it, do we *any* of us grow right up out of a need for an intermediate area between ourselves, with our personal inner world, and external or shared reality? The strain that the baby feels in sorting out the two is never altogether lost, and we allow ourselves a cultural life, something that can be shared, yet something that is personal. I refer, of course, to such things as friendship and the practice of religion. And in any case there are the senseless things we all do. For instance why do I smoke? For the answer I would have to go to an infant, who wouldn't laugh at me, I'm sure, because an infant knows better than anyone how silly it is always to be sensible.

It's strange, perhaps, but sucking a thumb or a rag doll may feel real, while a real feed may make for unreal feelings. The real feed touches off reflexes, and instincts get involved in a full-blooded way, and the infant has not yet got so far in the establishment of a self as to be able to encompass such powerful experiences. Doesn't this remind you of the riderless horse that wins the Grand National? This victory does not gain a prize for the owner because the jockey failed to keep his seat. The owner feels frustrated and the jockey may have been hurt. When you adapt yourselves to the personal needs and rhythms of your infant at the beginning you are enabling this starter in the race to keep his seat, even to ride his own horse, and to enjoy riding for riding's sake.

For the immature self of a very young child it is self-expression perhaps in the form of these odd habits like cloth-sucking that feels real to the infant, and that gives the mother and infant an opportunity for a human relatedness that is not at the mercy of the animal instincts.

[1956]

FOUR

Saying "No"

DONALD WOODS WINNICOTT

This programme and the next two form a series. The subject is "Saying 'No'." This evening you will hear a discussion between several mothers, and I shall make a brief comment at the end. Next week and the week after I will do most of the talking, but some extracts from the discussion will be quoted, just to remind you.

I think you will enjoy the discussion, which lasts about eight minutes. It feels real to me. As you listen you can be quite sure it isn't staged. It's just the way you would discuss the same subject.

The Mothers' Conversation

MOTHERS

"It's very difficult to draw the happy medium, whether you tell children not to do this, not to do that all the time, or whether you let them go the whole hog. But, on the other hand, you can't have your home completely wrecked."

"I've just acquired a new home, we've had a flat for a year and we had to buy everything for it, and the new baby as well. And I've decided just to let her have the freedom of the flat, and she's a happy baby because of that."

"Yes, but she's what—twenty months?"

"Twenty-one months, and very active." (*talking together*)

"Three years! Three years of age is slightly different from twenty months." (*talking together*)

"But I've decided to maintain that attitude."

"Will your child have the same freedom when she visits other people's houses?"

"At the moment she has, because she's extremely curious, which she would be at this age."

"I think the business of children being well-behaved when they visit other people depends largely on how much freedom they do have at home. Because if they have freedom to kick around and muck around, in one way or another, then they've not . . ."

"They're not so curious."

"Then they don't want to do it anywhere else. All right, the child will when you come home from shopping take the bag of rice—if you've foolishly left it there—and scatter it all over the floor. (*laughter*) The child's not being naughty, you've been stupid. I mean, when my child does that I realise that the quicker we get over to the sandpit again, where—you know—she can scatter as much as she likes, the better we'll be." (*talking together*)

"Doesn't she ever get bored with the sandpit, and the rice is more intriguing?"

"Of course it is, but also, I mean, well, puddles for instance. I've learned this lesson from somebody else, because my child was looked after for the first year, not full time, but during the days while I was still teaching (before

I had the second one I decided I wanted to go on teaching). But even in her ordinary shoes this lady would let her go into puddles, at certain times, and then say 'All right, this time you mustn't go into puddles, because you're just going out. I can't change you now.' And she wouldn't go in the puddles. And it's a very good lesson I've learned, that one. I mean, if you let the child do something when it's not going to be too much of a nuisance to you, then she won't do it when you sort of explain to her that there's a reason she shouldn't do it this time." (*talking together*)

"It doesn't get across, does it?" (*talking together*)

"It's no good just springing it, you must prepare them."

"You can make a game of the explanation: 'Let's do this,' and gently break away from whatever they're doing that's destructive, and find something else to do." (*talking together*) "Well I do . . . explain rationally. What I mean is this business of making a game of whatever the child is doing at the time, and introducing him to another game."

"Distraction?"

"Distraction, yes."

"I think it depends on not having too many things which you say 'No' about. I mean, when our first baby was very little there were two things we said 'No' about. One was some green plants we had in the living-room, we didn't want them pulled about, and the second was electrical wires, of which we had too many hanging around. We said 'No' about these; the rest—I mean if there was anything she could do damage to we put out of the way."

"The wisest thing." (*talking together*)

"These were 'No' always. And the rest weren't. So that when you said a new 'No' to something you knew for some reason she didn't understand, she didn't mind."

"I started the same with mine, with equal success."

"There are occasions when you can't avoid saying 'No.' At twenty-one months you can put things out of their reach—they probably can't climb. It does seem that plugs are things you cannot put out of the way."

"You should get proper plugs fitted—there are proper plugs for electrical appliances."

"I think you just decide that you say 'No' and stick to it. And that it's far better to be spanked by you than to give them an electric shock, or any other kind of shock."

"You can't, after all, always afford to have all the plugs moved." (*talking together*)

"I think it's not so easy as people make out to have a few 'No's' and stick to them. I think if you have a 'No' that seems important enough and interesting enough to the child it'll fascinate them just because it's the only 'No.' Take matches—they'll get a sort of thing that matches are the most interesting thing in the house because you've been so 'No' about them. I think—I think you've got to let them play with matches."

"Has anybody tried teaching them to strike matches by holding them away? . . ."

". . . but that fascinates all the more."

"I don't know, I think it's an awfully good approach, though, to show children just what does happen if they go on playing with them."

"Even to the extent of burning their fingers literally?"

"I don't know—I suppose that's a bit hard, but if they can get near enough to realise that it is hot and it could be painful and they can learn from other things what heat is."

"Yes, I was lucky; my child touched the towel rail once, and it was hot and it burnt him, and I said 'Hot'."

"My second child, he will do something and he will get hurt and he will realise, or I presume he realises, why he's been hurt; but the next day he's willing to go and do exactly the same thing again."

"It's a matter of temperament I'm sure. My first child took a mouthful of hot bacon at the age of about eighteen months, and I said 'Hot' and from then on I don't think she's ever burned herself. Because she knows what 'hot' is and she's lots of imagination and also quite frightened about it. But the second child's quite different. She's had lots and lots of mouthfuls of hot bacon."

"There are certain things they cannot do which don't exactly hurt them. Like an automatic lighting gas cooker. All my little boy has to do is lift up the lighter. Well it turns on the gas, it doesn't hurt him, it just lights up the gas and it can do a lot of damage to anything that happens to be above. He knows he shouldn't do it, and he shakes his head as he does it." (*laughter*)

"Well, isn't that where a well-timed slap comes in?"

"Isn't that surely where you have to be for rather a long time on the look-out, and the moment he gets near it you whip him away?" (*talking together*)

"It is the responsibility of the mother that a child just should not be in the kitchen, and that's that. I mean, it can only be our responsibility."

"But you're washing and cooking." (*talking together*)

"A child won't stay in its play-pen indefinitely."

"Oh no, I know, but I should have thought there was a way of getting over quite a lot of this. It's by distractions. If he goes to the gas flame, you give him something equally attractive but safe. It's the same way as with an older child, you just have to remind them all the time that they must turn the saucepan handles away, so that any younger child won't come and pull anything."

"We're rather fortunate. Our dining-room has a connecting door with the kitchen and the children have to have the dining-room as a sort of play-room, and I try to keep them in there. But I don't shut the door on them. And as long as they know that I'm just in the next room, and they can see me if they want to, they nearly always will stay in the dining-room."

"What age?"

"Oh, from the early stage, from the time they've been out of the play-pen, from about a year or so. They will come and see me round the door you know, and then they'll go back in again with all their toys and things."

"Do you think this constant being on the watch, and having to find distractions, and remind them and so on, is the most tiring thing?"

"Yes." (*talking together*)

"Added to which it's a matter of time. You're trying to do so many things at once, you're cooking, perhaps you're boiling up nappies, somebody knocks at the front door, and you suddenly turn round and find your little boy is playing with the gas taps, or he's trying to plug in an electric fire you forgot to take away the night before. That's the sort of thing that happens—you can't possibly think of everything in advance."

DWW

I expect this group of mothers went on discussing and exchanging views over a cup of tea. We have to leave them there.

This week, as I said earlier, I shall make only a brief general comment, and next week and the week after I hope to take up and develop some of the points raised. I always enjoy hearing this sort of thing, when people talk about their specialty. It's the same when farmers talk about wheat and rye and potatoes, or when any craftsman talks of his trade. For instance, these women talk of the difference between babies at twenty-four months or three years or any other age. They know what immense changes occur from month to month. At twelve months only a few words make sense to a baby as words, whereas at twenty-four months verbal explanations begin to be a good way of communicating, and an effectual method for getting co-operation when "No" is what you actually mean. We see from the discussion that there are several stages. I could sort out three. First, you are absolutely responsible all the time. Second, you begin to convey "No" to your baby because you are right in discerning the dawning of intelligence and the beginnings of your baby's ability to sort out what you allow from what you don't allow. You are not trying to deal with moral right and wrong, you are simply letting the infant know about the dangers that you protect him or her from. I think your "No's" are based on the idea of real dangers. Do you remember how two mothers talked about heat? At an appropriate moment they uttered the word "hot" and so linked up the danger with pain. But many dangers are not linked with pain in such a simple way, so "No" has to suffice until the next stage is reached. At the third stage you gain the infant's co-operation by offering an explanation. This involves language. "No" because it's hot. "No" because I say "No." "No" because I like that plant, implying that if the plant is pulled about you won't love the baby so much for a few minutes.

I have spoken about three stages, but these stages overlap. First, there is the stage at which you take full responsibility, so that if anything untoward happens you blame yourself, and this stage only very slowly becomes obsolete. In fact you continue to take responsibility, but you get some relief because of the child's growing ability to understand things. If this first stage ever becomes a thing of the past, this means your child has grown right up out of the need for family control and has become an independent member of society.

At the second stage you impose yourself and your view of the world on the infant. This stage will usually change over into the third stage of explanation, but the rate of change and the manner of it depends on the child as well as on you. Children are so different from each other in the way they develop. We can take up these points next week. Perhaps you already see that saying "No" isn't just saying "No."

❀   ❀   ❀

Last week you heard some mothers discussing saying "No," and I made a brief comment. This week and the next I shall talk about some of the things that I found myself thinking while I was listening. But there is something I would like to say that has to do with the whole discussion. In my work I learn a great deal about the difficulties that mothers have when they are not fortunately placed. Perhaps they have big personal difficulties so that they can't fulfil themselves even when they can see the way; or they have husbands who are away or who don't give proper support, or who interfere, who are even jealous; some have no husband but they still have to bring the baby up. And then there are others who are caught up in adverse conditions, poverty, crowded dwellings, unkind neighbours. So much so that they can't see the wood for the trees. And there are also those who are caring for other people's babies.

I feel that the mothers who met here to discuss the management of their own babies are of the usual run of healthy and fortunate people, and they have the sense of security which is necessary if they are to get down to the real problems of infant care. I know that most mothers are just like these that we heard, but I like to draw attention to the fact that they are happy, partly because we lose something if we take good fortune for granted, and partly because I am thinking of all the mothers who may be listening and who are inhibited, unhappy, frustrated and not succeeding; because everyone really wants to succeed.

After saying this I remind you of three stages I sorted out for you last time. First, I said, you are caught up in a process which in effect involves you as totally responsible for the protection of the infant. Then comes a time when you can say "No," and then comes a time for explanations.

About this first stage in which you are fully responsible, I would like to say a word. You will be able to say in a few months' time that you never, not once, let your infant down, though of course you had to be a frustrating person all along because you couldn't, nor could anyone, fulfil all of an infant's needs—a good job you don't have to. There is no "No," is there, in this first stage; and I reminded you that this first stage overlaps the subsequent stages; it goes on and on and on right up to the time when your child becomes grown-up, independent of family control. You will do awful things, but I don't think you will ever really let your child down, not if you can help it.

At the next stage, what I called stage two, "No" begins to appear. You convey "No" somehow or other. Perhaps you just say "Brhhhhhhh." Or you screw up your nose or frown. Or the use of the word "No" is quite a good way unless the infant is deaf. I think if you are happy you find it easy to do this "No" business on a practical basis, establishing a way of life that fits in with yours and with the world around. Unhappy mothers, out of their own unhappiness, may tend to overdo the happy loving side of infant care, and sometimes they say "No" just because they are irritable, but that just can't be helped. And following this is stage three, which I call the stage of explanations. Some people find it a great relief when they can at last talk and hope to be understood, but I am saying that the basis of everything surely is what happens earlier.

I would like to remind you now of the part of the discussion where a mother said she introduced "No's" one at a time. I think the point is that she was clear in her own mind what she would allow and what she would not allow. If she had been in a muddle herself, the baby would have lost something valuable. Listen again to a fragment of the mothers' conversation:

MOTHERS

"I think it depends on not having too many things which you say 'No' about. I mean, when our first baby was very little there were two things we said 'No' about. One was some green plants we had in the living-room, we didn't want them pulled about, and the second was electrical wires, of which we had too many hanging around. We said 'No' about these; the rest—I mean if there was anything she could do damage to we put out of the way."

"The wisest thing." (*talking together*)

"These were 'No' always. And the rest weren't. So that when you said a new 'No' to something you knew for some reason she didn't understand, she didn't mind."

"I started the same with mine, with equal success."

DWW

So here we are told of a mother's capacity to adapt to the infant's need for an uncomplicated start to something which must needs become more and more complex. The infant had two "No's" at first, and then no doubt others were added, and there was no unnecessary muddle.

Then let's remind ourselves of the way a word was used before explanation could be given in words. Here in this bit the word "hot" brings us just exactly between stages two and three, as I call them.

MOTHERS

"Even to the extent of burning their fingers literally?"

"I don't know—I suppose that's a bit hard, but if they can get near enough to realise that it is hot and it could be painful and they can learn from other things what heat is."

"Yes, I was lucky; my child touched the towel rail once, and it was hot and it burnt him, and I said 'Hot'."

"My second child, he will do something and he will get hurt and he will realise, or I presume he realises, why he's been hurt; but the next day he's willing to go and do exactly the same thing again."

"It's a matter of temperament I'm sure. My first child took a mouthful of hot bacon at the age of about eighteen months, and I said 'Hot' and from then on I don't think she's ever burned herself. Because she knows what 'hot' is and she's lots of imagination and also quite frightened about it. But the second child's quite different. She's had lots and lots of mouthfuls of hot bacon."

"There are certain things they cannot do which don't exactly hurt them. Like an automatic lighting gas cooker. All my little boy has to do is lift up the lighter. Well it turns on the gas, it doesn't hurt him, it just lights up the gas and it can do a lot of damage to anything that happens to be above. He knows he shouldn't do it, and he shakes his head as he does it." (*laughter*)

"Well, isn't that where a well-timed slap comes in?"

DWW

... Well, perhaps it does. You can see from the way they talk that it is in the living experience from moment to moment that all the important work is done. There are no lessons and there is no set time for learning. The lesson comes with the way the people concerned find themselves reacting.

I want to repeat, however, nothing absolves the mother of babies and small children from her task of eternal vigilance.

MOTHERS

"All right, the child will when you come home from shopping take the bag of rice—if you've foolishly left it there—and scatter it all over the floor. (*laughter*) The child's not being naughty, you've been stupid. I mean, when my child does that I realise that the quicker we get over to the sandpit again, where—you know—she can scatter as much as she likes, the better we'll be."

DWW

Yes, it was her fault that the rice got spilled, wasn't it! But I guess she was annoyed though! Sometimes it's just a matter of architecture, the way rooms are arranged or a glass panel in the door between the kitchen and the child's playroom.

MOTHERS

"We're rather fortunate. Our dining-room has a connecting door with the kitchen and the children have to have the dining-room as a sort of play-room, and I try to keep them in there. But I don't shut the door on them. And as long as they know that I'm just in the next room, and they can see me if they want to, they nearly always will stay in the dining-room."

"What age?"

"Oh, from the early stage, from the time they've been out of the play-pen, from about a year or so. They will come and see me round the door you know, and then they'll go back in again with all their toys and things."

DWW

Yes, she was fortunate, wasn't she, in the way her rooms were arranged?

And then we hear of the strain that eternal vigilance puts on mothers. This is especially true, I think, when the woman, before she was married, had a regular job, so that she knew the satisfaction that most men know in their work, that of being able to concentrate, and then to come home and relax. Isn't the world a bit unfair to women over this? Let's hear what the group says about this.

MOTHERS

"Do you think this constant being on the watch, and having to find distractions, and remind them and so on, is the most tiring thing?"

"Yes." (*talking together*)

"Added to which it's a matter of time. You're trying to do so many things at once, you're cooking, perhaps you're boiling up nappies, somebody knocks at the front door, and you suddenly turn round and find your little boy is playing with the gas taps, or he's trying to plug in an electric fire you forgot to take away the night before. That's the sort of thing that happens—you can't possibly think of everything in advance."

DWW

No, you certainly can't. Fortunately, eternal vigilance is not eternal, though it feels so. It only lasts for a limited time for each child. Too soon the infant is a toddler, the toddler is going to school, and vigilance is then something shared with the teachers. However, "No" remains an important word in the parents' vocabulary, and prohibiting remains a part of what mothers and fathers find themselves doing right on and until each child in his or her own way breaks out of the parental control and establishes a personal way of life and of living.

But there are some important things in this discussion which I have not yet had time to refer to, so I am glad to have the chance to continue next week.

❋   ❋   ❋

This week I shall go on discussing saying "No," in infant and child care. I shall do as I did before and talk about three stages, because this is a convenient way to go about developing the theme of when and how to say "No" and why. I want to describe the three stages again, but in a rather different language, so in a way it won't matter if you didn't hear last week or if you have forgotten all about it.

I did say of the three stages that they overlap. Stage one doesn't end when stage two begins, and so on. Stage one comes before you say "No"; the baby doesn't understand yet, and you are absolutely in charge, and you ought to be. You take full responsibility, and this taking of responsibility lessens but never quite ends until the child becomes grown-up, that is to say finished with the need for the controls that the family provides.

This that I call the first stage really belongs to the parental attitude, and father (if he exists and if he is around) soon takes part in the setting up and the maintaining of this parental attitude. I will go on to the next two stages later; they have to do with words and the first stage hasn't to do with words at all. So at first the mother, soon the two parents, can make it their job to see that unexpected things don't happen. They can do this deliberately, but it mainly happens in their bodies almost; it's a whole mode of behaviour that reflects a mental attitude. The baby feels secure and absorbs the mother's confidence in herself just like taking in milk. During all this time the parents are saying "No," they are saying "No" *to the world*, they say "No, keep off, keep out of our circle; in our circle is the thing we care for and we allow nothing past the barrier." If the parent becomes frightened then something has got past the barrier and the baby is hurt, just as much as if a terrible noise has got through and given the baby a sensation so acute that it's unbearable. In air-raids babies weren't afraid of bombs, but they were affected immediately when their mothers developed panic. But most infants come through the early months without ever having suffered in this way, and when eventually the world has to break through the barriers, then the growing child has begun to develop ways of dealing with the unexpected, and has even begun to be able to predict. We could talk about the various defences that the developing child acquires, but that would be another discussion altogether.

Out of this early phase in which you assume that you are responsible comes the sense of parental responsibility—the thing that distinguishes parents from children and perhaps makes nonsense of the game some people like to play whereby mother and father hope to be just pals to their children. But mothers have to be able at last to begin to let their infants know something of the dangers that they protect them from, and also to let them know what sort of behaviour would affect the mother's loving and liking. So they find themselves saying "No."

We can now see the second stage starting, when instead of saying "No" to the world around, the mother says "No" to her child. This has been referred to as introducing the reality principle, but it doesn't matter what it's called; the mother with her husband gradually introduces the infant to reality and reality to the infant. One way is by prohibition. You will be glad to hear me saying this, that saying "No" is one way, because prohibition is only one of two ways. The basis of "No" is "Yes." There are some babies who get brought up on the basis of "No." The mother perhaps feels that safety lies only in her pointing out innumerable danger situations. But it's unfortunate when the infant has to get to know the world this way. Quite a big proportion of infants can use the other method. Their expanding world has a relation to the increasing number of objects and kinds of objects about which mother is able to say "Yes." The infant's development in that case has more to do with what the mother allows than with what she prohibits. "Yes" forms the background on which "No" is added. This of course cannot entirely cover what has to be done; it's merely a matter of whether the infant is developing chiefly along one line or the other. Babies can be highly suspicious from early days, and I must remind you that there are all kinds of babies; but most of them are able to trust their mothers for a while at least. On the whole they reach out for things and for food that they have found mother approves of. Isn't it true that the whole of the first stage is one big "Yes"? It's "Yes" because you never let the baby down. You never really slip up on your over-all task. This is a great big unspoken "Yes" and it gives a firm basis for the infant's life in the world.

I know it's more complex. Soon each infant becomes aggressive and develops destructive ideas, and then naturally the baby's easy trusting of the mother is interfered with, and at times she doesn't feel friendly to the child at all, even though she remains her usual self. But we needn't deal with this sort of complication here, because we have plenty to think about when we see how complex the world quickly becomes in reality, in external reality. For instance, the mother has one set of don'ts, and the helpful grandmother has another set, or there may be a nurse. Also mothers are not all scientists; they have all sorts of beliefs which couldn't be proved. You could find a mother, for instance, who fears that anything green is poisonous, so musn't be put to the mouth. Now how is a baby to know that a green object is poisonous and a yellow one is lovely? And what if the baby is colour-blind? I know a baby who was cared for by two people, one left-handed and the other right-handed, and this was too much. So we expect complications, but somehow infants come through; they come through to the third stage of explanation. They can then gather wisdom from the store of our knowledge; they can learn what we think we know, and the best thing is that they are now near to being able to disagree with the reasons we give.

To go over what I have said again, at first it's a matter of infant care and dependence, something rather like faith. Then it's a matter of morals; mother's version of morality has to do till the infant develops a personal morality. And then, with the explanations, there is at last a basis for understanding, and understanding is science and philosophy. Isn't it interesting to see the beginnings of big things like these already at this very early stage?

One more word about a mother's "No." Isn't this the first sign of father? In part fathers are like mothers and they can baby-sit and do all sorts of things like a woman. But as fathers, they seem to me to appear first on the infant's horizon as the hard thing in mother which enables her to say "No" and stick to it. Gradually and with luck this "No" principle becomes embodied in the man himself, Daddy, who becomes loved, and even liked, and who can administer the occasional slap without losing anything. But he has to earn the right to slap if he is going to slap, and to earn it by things like being around and by not being on the child's side against the mother. At first you may not like the idea of the embodiment of "No," but perhaps you will accept what I mean a little when I remind you that small children like being told "No." They don't want to play with soft things all the time; they like stones and sticks and the hard floor, and they like to be told where to get off as well as being cuddled.

[1960]

FIVE

Jealousy

DWW

What do you think about jealousy? Is it good or bad? Normal or abnormal? It would be a good idea when listening to the discussion which follows, between mothers of small children, to keep in mind this question each time when some manifestation of jealousy is described. Is this what is to be expected, or is something wrong somewhere? I think the answer has to be a complex one, but there is no point in making it more complex than need be, so we first of all chose parts of the discussion which are about the sort of things that go on in every home. I don't mind saying in advance that in my opinion jealousy is normal and healthy. Jealousy arises out of the fact that children love. If they have no capacity to love, then they don't show jealousy. Later on we shall have to look at the less healthy aspects of jealousy, and especially at the hidden kind. I think you will see that in the stories that these mothers tell us, jealousy usually comes to a natural end, although it perhaps starts up again and disappears again. Eventually healthy children become able to say they are jealous, and this gives them a chance to discuss what they are jealous about, and that may help a bit. I am putting forward the idea that the first thing to be said about jealousy is that it represents an achievement in the infant's development, indicating a capacity to love.

Further achievements enable the child to tolerate being jealous. The first jealousies are usually around the arrival of a new baby, and it is well-known that jealousy is not avoided by there being only one child in the family. Anything that takes up the mother's time can bring about jealousy, just as a baby can. I really do believe that children who have met jealousy and come to terms with it are richer for the experience. This is what I think, and now I suggest that we listen to some mothers answering questions and talking about jealousy.

MOTHERS

"Mrs. S. you've got, I know, eight children. Have any of them been jealous of each other?"

"Two or three of them have. The first baby was fifteen months when the second one was born and I was feeding the baby when he was about three weeks old and the child was stroking his hair and saying 'ba-ba' so lovingly and I said, 'Yes, isn't he sweet?', and the next minute the voice changed and the expression changed and he cracked him over the head and said 'ba-ba' and I began to think that the child wasn't quite happy about the baby. And a week later I was getting my hat on to go out and something made me look out of the window, and the baby was just about to be thrown on the path, so I switched that around promptly by putting him back in his old place and putting the baby in the handlebar place, and I've done that with them all and I found that there is no more trouble in the pram, they don't like being put out. And that child—the first one—made scenes and cried an awful lot and stamped his feet and I think it was because of the baby."

"Is he still jealous?"

"Not at all. He has got right out of that. He is the eldest one now and he is very proud of them all, but he was for a time."

"Mrs. L., what happened with your three?"

"Well, the eldest was two when his brother was born, and three-and-a-half when his sister was born. He was an easy, happy child, and on first seeing his brother he just took no notice at all. We tried to prepare him for the event. He just didn't understand."

"No, he was a bit young I suppose."

"Too young to understand. And his indifference lasted a week or two and then the day came when he saw the baby in the pram and he hadn't himself been in the pram for months because he was too big, but he wept bitterly."

"The baby was how old by then?"

"Oh, about three or four weeks, and he wept bitterly, and that was the beginning I think. And after that each time the baby was changed he would instantly be either wet or dirty and it took a long time for him to improve. And it was just when he was older and understood that he improved about that."

"What happened when his sister was born?"

"He always treated her with great love and affection, and so did the second boy."

"No other sort of lapses from any of them?"

"No. But later on he became aggressive when his brother began to sit up and take notice."

"You think that was a jealousy sign, do you?"

"Oh, definitely, yes. One day I found him trying to suffocate the baby in the pram, and he was most spiteful with him. And I'm afraid I used to retaliate at times on the baby's behalf, because I just couldn't bear it. But I don't think that was a good thing. It didn't improve matters at all."

DWW

These seem to me to be everyday family matters. I will remind you of the ages of the children, because the age makes such a difference. The boy who stroked the baby's hair while the baby was being fed, and then proceeded to try to throw him out onto the path, was fifteen months old when the baby was born. And then there was the two-year-old who at first seemed indifferent. He had been told what to expect, but perhaps he could not understand. It was three weeks after his brother's birth when he saw the baby in the pram that had once been his that he wept bitterly. He got over this with sympathetic help from the mother, but later when his brother began to sit up and take notice, he became aggressive and spiteful, and on one occasion he tried to suffocate the baby, in the pram. Not till he was about four did he come round to a more friendly attitude. Neither he nor his brother were jealous of the baby sister. Here is some more of the mothers' discussion:

MOTHERS

"Mrs. T, what about jealousies among your seven?"

"Well, the only jealousy I find has been among the girls."

"How many girls have you got?"

"There's only two, you see—there's a boy, then a girl, then four boys and then the other girl. And Jean used to ask and ask and ask, you know, 'Can we have a baby sister?' Each time it was a baby boy, and she got a bit ratty for a day or two, but it soon blew over. Well, then, she came in from school one day and discovered she had got a baby sister, and she seemed absolutely thrilled at first. The trouble was I had the baby on the 10th, Jean's seventh birthday was on the 16th—no party, I couldn't do it. So for about a month Jean came in from school every evening, had her tea and went straight to bed crying her eyes out. We couldn't do anything with her, she wouldn't listen, but I did think she'd got over it, you know—I did think I'd got her round that. But yesterday baby was ill in bed, and I said to Jean, as innocent as you please, 'Jean would you go and get me a nightgown for Patricia?' And Jean just turned round and said, 'No, why should I? Let her go and get it herself— she's big enough now.'"

"She's going on being jealous?"

"Yes, it looks like it. But it's been all very peaceful since Patricia was about six weeks. Now she's gone two, and it's suddenly come out again. I can only hope that we can get rid of it again now."

"Jean isn't in any way jealous of her brothers?"

"No."

D W W

It was a week before Jean's seventh birthday that her baby sister was born, and when she had to do without her birthday party she became violently jealous. This first bout

of jealousy lasted six weeks, and it all started up again when
she was nine and her sister was two. Jean hadn't minded
the arrival of four boy babies in this family of seven, and
she had indeed always asked for a sister. I suppose the sister you actually get isn't necessarily the same as the sister
you long for.

Now here is one more story:

MOTHERS

"Mrs. G., what about yours? Have you had any jealousies?"

"Yes, we did have. My little girl who's four-and-a-half, she
was just coming up to three when the little boy was born
and she was very thrilled to have a baby brother, or anyhow,
to have a baby. But we found, almost from the word 'go,'
that if I had the baby then she had to go and sit on my husband's knee or vice versa; she wanted me to read to her
while I was feeding the baby, or at least sit beside me."

"And did that work out?"

"That did, yes. The jealousy phase blew over, faded out,
and was quiet until her little brother was—what, I suppose
about a year old or so, when he was up and about and in
the play-pen and so on, and we had rather a lot of trouble
over toys. I brought out her baby toys for him, and of
course she recognised them, and 'That's mine, that's mine,
that's mine.' And all this business of going back to play
with baby toys, and I found I had to get some more baby
toys that were exclusively his, otherwise there was no
quietness about."

"She didn't want to play with those?"

"No, no, no, she wouldn't touch his, but if she saw him

playing with hers, even though she hadn't touched them for about two years, she wanted them again. And that again faded out, without anything very violent happening. Now he's eighteen months, and it's come up again, this time because he's on the move and he's after her things."

"... tugs of war over them?"

"Yes, we do, indeed. She'll get her things set up—I'm always telling her, 'Put them on the table where he can't reach,' but she'll put them down somewhere low, and she just turns her back and he'll come along and start moving them all over the place. She gets really wild—but she's very patient with him, really."

D W W

This little girl was just nearly three when her brother was born. She was thrilled about it, but she felt displaced by the baby when he was actually there on his mother's knee, and she went to her father instead. When the baby was a year old and she was four, she began to resent the baby's claim on her toys. Even toys that she had seemed to be finished with. Do you notice that she put her toys where the baby could reach them? Her mother says she is very patient with her brother much of the time, and I get the feeling that she really does like him to get at her toys, though she protests; she perhaps feels from his point of view as well as from her own.

Now that you have heard all these stories, do you feel as I do that these jealousies are part of healthy family life?

❀   ❀   ❀

I have been asking myself the question: How and when does jealousy start? And what is it that has to be there before the word jealousy or envy can begin to be used and make sense? I bring in the word envy because jealousy and envy are very closely linked, for a child who is jealous of a new baby envies the baby his or her possession of the mother's attention. I notice that those mothers who were talking about their babies did not happen to talk about jealousy in any child under fifteen months old. I wonder what you would say about this? I think that evidence of jealousy or envy might be detected earlier than at fifteen months, but not very much earlier. At nine months, for instance, a baby would be too young, too immature as a person to be jealous. At a year probably not; possibly occasionally; but at fifteen months certainly yes. Gradually as the children get older so jealousy is about more complex things, but at the beginning it is fairly obviously about a relationship that is disturbed, or about a threat to a possession which stands for a relationship. It is the relationship to the mother that is at the basis of jealousy, and this comes to include the relationship to the father as time goes on. We find that many of the earliest jealousies are obviously about mother, and they often centre round feeding. This is because for the infant at the beginning feeding is such a vital thing. For the mother feeding is only one of the many things she does for her baby, but to her too it may be very important. Here is part of the discussion between some of the mothers.

MOTHERS

"There's twenty-two months between them and when the second one was born—I had the second one at home—and my little boy saw him when he was a few minutes old, more or less, that was all right for a few days. Then he happened to see me feeding, and from that time on, for a couple of months, he stood and screamed every time I fed the baby, and there was nothing I could do. I tried everything to try and pacify that child and give him all the comfort I could, but it's very difficult when you're feeding a child, and he just stood and screamed. But after about two months he got over it and he seemed to get over his jealousy altogether, and then when the child—the second one began to sit up about seven or eight months—we had the same performance all over again, not the screaming but jealousy."

"Yes, mine was a bit younger; I must say I find it quite intriguing that she's not had a bottle for—oh some time—she'd forgotten how to suck. I was staggered at this because she came up and she—when I was feeding the little one and she wanted to have a go too, so I thought, good—but she didn't, she—as soon as she got near it she was sort of a bit revolted by it. I thought, all right, have a go if you want to, see what happens—and she came up several times—she's done it fairly recently, just as a sort of joke. I didn't put her off at all, I said, 'Come on, have a go,' and she didn't want it. But she has now taken to having a bottle as the baby is now on a bottle, and I give her a nasty little one, poor child, a tiny little thing, but as a token, you know."

"My elder daughter sits on my lap while the baby is feeding, and I'm breast-feeding so you can imagine it's all rather a shambles. (*laughter*) She adores it you know, she pats the baby's head and strokes it . . . but then she's only seventeen months you see, so it's rather different."

"We've had jealousy with the two eldest ones, not with the second and third; but the first two, my little girl, when the second one arrived, she wanted to go on my husband's lap or she wanted to have something special or she wanted me to read to her while I was feeding the baby and that sort of thing, and then the phase went off and now the little boy is seventeen months and we do have these awful wars. Whatever one or the other has, the other wants, and the little boy now—of course there was a time when she could take anything from him, she is three years older than he is—but now he gets a jolly good hold on whatever he's got, and yells—doesn't cry but really yells fiercely at her. But they're both of them very fond of the baby in their gestures and so on, and they don't either of them seem to be jealous of the latest one."

"That isn't in fact jealousy surely when they just fight over possessions, is it . . ."

"It's because they want my attention."

"Oh, I see."

"You see, a baby toy which I will give to the little boy— something which the little girl has completely grown out of—because I've given it to him she will then immediately want it; and if I hadn't given it to the little boy, if I'd just left it lying on the table where she could have reached it if she'd wanted it, she wouldn't have taken any notice at all."

DWW

From this you can see that quite a lot has to do with the feeds. I can use the last bit of the conversation to illustrate what I want to say. I am thinking of the little girl who is often openly jealous of the second baby, which was a boy, and this wore off. And then she and the boy, who is now seventeen months old, have these awful wars over toys. But it's different the way she is jealous and the way he just hangs on and yells. One mother said: "That isn't jealousy, it's just a fight over possessions." And I agree, but it's exactly here that we can look at the way jealousy develops. I said that there is an age for jealousy. Now I want to say that after a certain age the child is jealous and before that age the child is just hanging on to a possession. First is possessing, and jealousy comes later.

I can't help being reminded of a theatre agency which advertises with the following slogan: "You want the best seats; we have them." This always makes me madly jealous so that I feel like rushing off to get the seats that I want and they have. The snag is that I have to pay for them. Using this as an illustration, I can say that up to a certain age a little boy or girl is all the time proclaiming: "I have the best mother"—only not in those words. Eventually the moment comes when the child can proclaim: "I have the best mother—you want her." This is a painful new development.

To get a clear sequence of events, we must go back a little further, though. There is a time before the baby is, so to speak, proclaiming: "I have the best mother." In this earlier stage this fact of the best mother is assumed. There is no place for advertisement. The mother, and everything that stands for her, is taken for granted by the infant. Then comes: "I have the best mother," and this marks the dawn of the baby's understanding that the mother is not just part

of the baby's self, but that she comes to the baby from outside, and she might not come, and there could be other
mothers. For the baby the mother now becomes a possession, and one that can be held on to or dropped. All this has
to wait for development in the little child, what we call
emotional growth. And then comes the second half of the
slogan: "and you want her." But this is not jealousy yet, it is
a matter of a defended possession. Here the child clings on
tight. If the theatre did this we wouldn't be able to get to
the theatre. Then at last comes the recognition that the
central possession, mother, can belong to someone else.
The child is now one of the people who want and is no
longer one of those who have. It is somebody else who has.
This is when jealousy becomes the right word to use to describe the changes that happen in a child when a new infant
appears like a ghost of a past self, feeding at the breast, or
sleeping peacefully in the pram.

I will repeat what I have said. I have referred to early infancy in which what is desirable is part of the self, or it
makes an appearance as if created out of the infant's need.
The coming and going is taken for granted by the baby.
Then the thing or person who is loved becomes part of a
world outside the infant, and is a possession to be held or
lost. Any threat of loss of ownership leads to distress and to
a fierce clinging on to the object. In the course of time and
further development, the infant becomes the one who
threatens, the one who hates anything new that turns up to
claim the mother's attention, such as a new baby or perhaps
just the book she is reading. It can now be said that jealousy
has been achieved. The child envies the new baby or book,
and makes every effort to regain the position lost, even if

only for a time or in token form. So at the first times of jealousy it is common for us to see children trying to revert to
being infants, even if only in some way or for a little while.
They may even want to re-experience a breast-feed. But
commonly they long to be just treated as they were treated
when they had full possession, when they were the ones
who had, and they knew of no-one who had not, but
wanted. You may remember from the discussion in last
week's programme the child who started wetting again, and
you've just heard about the older one to whom the mother
gave a little bottle; it was a token, she said.

When you think of all that goes on in the little child
while the days and the weeks pass by, you can easily see
why there is a need for a reliable environment, and this is
the very thing that you can give your child better than anyone else can. You often wonder, is something right or
wrong? But it is more interesting to see things in terms of
the child's growth and development.

The stories in the discussion show that jealousy tends to
disappear, and I want to examine how this happens. What
happens depends on the development that is all the time
going on in the child. I think you like to know what sort of
things do go on in the child, just as a matter of interest.
When things go wrong, as they must do from time to time,
you are at a disadvantage if you are working blind. If you
know what's going on you become less sensitive to criticism
and to chance remarks from passers-by.

I want to speak of three ways in which things going on in
the child enable jealousy to come to an end. The first is

this. Jealousy is what we see when the child is in a state of acute conflict. It might be just anxiety, except that the child knows what it is about. The jealous child is actually experiencing loving and hating, both at once, and it feels horrible. Let us think of the child. At first, perhaps, even for the child it looks rather nice to see the new baby being nursed or fed. Gradually it dawns, however, that this is not oneself but another who is there, and the love of the mother produces extreme anger, anger with the new baby, with mother, or just with everything. For a time the child only knows anger. Some of the anger gets expressed. The child screams; perhaps kicks; or hits; or makes a mess. Imaginatively everything is spoilt, broken, destroyed. Surely the thing that brings about the new development is the survival of the world, of the baby, of the mother. The new development is the child's recognition of this survival. This is just one more way in which the small child begins to sort out fantasy from fact. In the child's imagination the world was destroyed by the anger, as by an atom bomb, but it survives, and the mother's attitude is unchanged.

So it's safe, then, to imaginatively destroy, to hate. And with this new thing to help, the child becomes able to be contented with only doing a little of the screaming and hitting and kicking that would surely be appropriate.

In a few weeks the jealousy has settled down to something else, the experience of going on loving, with the love complicated by ideas of destruction. The result for us who are watching is that we see a child who is sometimes sad. It's sad to love something or someone and to dream that what one loves comes to harm.

Further relief comes from the fact that in destructive dreams the thing hurt can be something standing for the baby or the mother, perhaps a cat, or a dog, or a chair. Along with the child's sadness comes some degree of concern for the baby or whatever it was that was the object of jealousy. But mothers know they can't at first rely on the child's concern because, for a time, concern all too readily changes over to a jealous attack, and if no-one is about harm is done.

My point here is that the imaginative life begins to function, and to offer the child relief from the need for direct action, and this gives time and opportunity for the beginnings in the child of a sense of responsibility. The second way that I think jealousy can end is through the growing power of the child to absorb satisfactory experiences and make them part of the self. There grows up an accumulation of good memories in the child, memories of being cared for well; memories of nice sensations; of being bathed; of yelling; or smiling; of finding things just when and where they were expected, even better than they could have been expected. And also there is a building up of memories of satisfactions following orgies of excitement, especially feeding.

All these things could be added up and called an idea of mother or of mother and father. There is a reason why jealousy often doesn't appear at all in a child, because the child has had enough, enough at any rate to be able to spare a little.

The third thing is rather more complicated. It has to do with a child's ability to live through the experiences of others. We call this stepping into the other person's shoes. But this expression seems a bit funny when the other person is an infant feeding at the breast or being bathed or lying asleep in a cot. However do small children become able to do this? Some do take a long time, even years, before they let themselves not only see the other person's point of view but actually enjoy an extra bit of life that the other person is living. It is easy to see children—boys as well as girls—identifying themselves with their mothers. They let the mother be the actual mother while they play at being in her place, imagining themselves into her position. Here is a bit of the discussion which illustrates this:

MOTHERS

"Mrs. G., what about the new baby in your family?"

"Well, neither of them—neither of the elder ones—have shown any jealousy towards the new baby, but they have shown jealousy, both of them, towards each other about touching the baby or fondling the baby or holding the baby."

"A sort of rivalry?"

"Yes, rivalry between them. Say I'm sitting down and I have the baby on my lap and the little girl comes over to talk to the baby. Immediately the eighteen-month-old will come charging over and try to elbow her out of the way, before she gets a look in. And from that point a sort of tug-of-war starts as to who's going to have the baby."

"What do you do?"

"Well, in that case I put a protective arm around the baby and see that they move up a few inches, to give him breathing space."

"Is that a common occurrence?"

"Yes, I think so . . . starting pulling the baby, 'It's my turn to hold the baby,' or 'It's her turn.' He's too young to leave with them, this small babe on my lap. It comes to a case of both sit down, I give it to one without letting go of it, and I count up to ten: 'Right, now the next one.' It's a good idea, but it doesn't really work."

DWW

Here is another example in which a little girl seems to identify herself with her baby brother:

MOTHERS

"The jealousy phase blew over, faded out, and was quiet until her little brother was—what, I suppose about a year old or so, when he was up and about and in the play-pen and so on, and we had rather a lot of trouble over toys. I brought out her baby toys for him, and of course she recognised them, and 'That's mine, that's mine, that's mine.' And all this business of going back to play with baby toys, and I found I had to get some more baby toys that were exclusively his, otherwise there was no quietness about."

"She didn't want to play with those?"

"No, no, no, she wouldn't touch his, but if she saw him playing with hers, even though she hadn't touched them for about two years, she wanted them again. And that again faded out, without anything very violent happening. Now he's eighteen months, and it's come up again, this time because he's on the move and he's after her things."

". . . tugs of war over them?"

"Yes, we do, indeed. She'll get her things set up—I'm always telling her, 'Put them on the table where he can't reach,' but she'll put them down somewhere low, and she just turns her back and he'll come along and start moving them all over the place. She gets really wild—but she's very patient with him, really."

DWW

When we used this in our first jealousy programme I said: "I get the feeling that this little girl really does like her baby brother to get at her toys, though she protests." I added: "Perhaps she feels from his point of view as well as from her own." Great enrichment comes from the ability to imaginatively live through the experience of others if this can be done without loss of the sense of what is strictly the experience of the self. Here is one of the ways that playing starts up, and in imaginative play there is no limit to this process of identifying oneself with people and things. The child can be a vacuum cleaner or a horse; can be a queen or a prince; or can be the new baby; or the mother feeding the baby; or the father. We can't make a child able to play, but by protecting and tolerating and waiting and by hundreds of things you do without thinking you are facilitating the child's development. There is a lot more that could be said, but perhaps this is enough to show that when jealousy disappears this is because of the development that has taken place in the child made possible by consistent good care.

✳   ✳   ✳

I have talked about jealousy as a healthy, normal thing in small children, something that means that they love, and that they have already made considerable progress in their journey away from the complete immaturity that they

started with. Also I have talked about some of the developments in each child which makes it possible for jealousy to
stop being a feature. All the time I have made a point of
saying that these developments in the infant and small
child cannot take place satisfactorily without the thing that
you can provide, the living relationship in which the child
finds a live kind of reliability, one which depends on your
being what you are.

Along with this general thing that you provide, there are
some special things which you do which make a difference.
For instance, you help your child to predict what is going to
happen. When you know a big change must take place in
the infant's life, you try to give some warning. If you add a
new food, you give a taste, and then leave well alone, and
probably soon the baby will want the new thing that you
have ready. In the same way you try to give warning when
you are fairly well on in your new pregnancy, and you feel
sure you will be having a new baby. You might think it must
be easier if you can use words, if you can explain, but I
doubt this. Naturally if the child is already understanding
language, you do explain in words and stories, and with the
help of picture books. It would be funny if you didn't. But
the thing that makes the difference is your attitude, and
your attitude affects the issue long before language can be
used. If, for instance, a new pregnancy seems to you pleas-
antly natural, you can gradually let your year-old child know
that there is a reason why sitting on your lap isn't quite the
same as it was. Your little boy or girl gets to feel that you
have something in there that is important. If you happen to
be someone who does not easily accept the fact of pregnancy

and the changes it brings (and there are plenty of people like that), then there will grow up some mystery, and the small child whose life is about to be very much altered by the birth of a new baby will be in no way prepared when the new baby actually arrives. It is easier when the child who is affected is a bit older. Listen to this:

MOTHERS

"I was very anxious when I had Roger. You see, I had the two girls, fourteen and thirteen, and I wanted another child while I still could have one, and I was very perplexed about what to do about it, so I talked it over with the girls and said, how would they welcome the idea of me having another baby? And—which is an odd thing to do, isn't it, before you even conceive a child, to discuss it with your others, but I thought it wasn't a bad idea. And they were thrilled to bits, and thought it was a lovely thing, and they'd love to have a child, a baby. And so we all decided it would be a boy. And Susan, my younger daughter, then thirteen—Roger was premature and I told the midwife that I'd started labour—would she let Susan know, and if she'd like to come in and watch labour, she could do so. And she came bouncing in before school, and I was in the throes, you see, so I said, 'Well'—taking a deep breath and thinking I could ruin this child for life—'Well, this is a labour pain, and this is how you go on about it.' And she gave me a hearty smack on the back and said, 'Well, I expect you've got hours of it yet.' You know. 'See you after school,' and off she went. So she's now going to have her own baby next month, and I think she's thoroughly enjoying it. Well prepared, I should think."

DWW

That girl was thirteen, and of course the mother talked to her, but I think it was the mother's attitude that counted. What about younger children? Children of one or two years are a long way from understanding why there are twenty-nine days in February this year, and yet it is quite possible for them, isn't it, at one or two, to feel themselves a little bit into the position of being the mother of a baby? I am talking about feelings rather than about the child's mind. Most children by one year have some object that is very special to them, and which they sometimes nurse in a crude sort of way, and quite soon they are obviously playing at mothers and babies.

I said that you help your child to predict. There are other things you do; for instance, you try to be fair, and this is very difficult; you can only try. And you can hope that you haven't got a big favourite; except, of course, the new baby at the beginning who needs to feel that he has all of you. You and the child's father share your responsibility in all sorts of ways. And it is to the father that the child naturally turns when dissatisfied with mother and her new preoccupation. Most fathers would like to be a help, and they hate to be so much out at work that they are of no practical use.

And then again, on the whole you do not find yourself giving the precious objects of other children to the new baby, but you let each baby start afresh collecting objects and specialising. So although the main developments which are going on in the child are made possible because the child can rely on you, there are also many things that you do to meet special moments of stress.

You do know, I expect, that tremendous feelings are involved, and that in fact little children don't feel things less than we do. I wonder whether they don't feel things more. We grown-up people count ourselves lucky if we have found ways of keeping in touch with some of the intensity of experience that belongs to early childhood. Small children not only feel things with the utmost intensity, but also they can't be distracted from the actual thing that's bothering them. They haven't yet had time to organise personal methods for dealing with or for warding off feelings that are too painful, so that's why they yell; and that's why it makes so much difference when you can help your small child to predict anything that is going to happen that is out of the ordinary.

In the period of waiting for a predicted event, some arrangement of defences can become set up within the child's personality. Rather like what you see on your table when your children are playing soldiers and are arranging armies to defend or to attack a fort. The idea that the feelings of little children are very intense, and that anxieties and conflicts are so painful for them that they have to organise within themselves defences leads me on to the last thing that I want to say in this talk about jealousy. This has to do with abnormal jealousy. It often happens that things go wrong. Either jealousy doesn't cease, and continues as open jealousy, or else it goes under the counter, so to speak, and distorts the child's personality.

In the bringing up of children there is no point in aiming at perfection. Much that goes wrong mends in time; or mends well enough so that it doesn't show. But some does not mend. When I said and repeated several times that jealousy is normal and healthy, I was talking about young children. In the growth and development of the personality, there comes about in each boy or girl an ability to tolerate feeling jealous, to keep quiet about it, and to use it as a spur for action. If your friend has got something better than you have, you can fairly easily wait; perhaps you will catch up with her later, or perhaps you will be glad you bought something else instead. You weigh things up. I expect there are plenty of things about you that other people envy. It's all part of life and of people living together.

You grew up to manage these things fairly easily, but you started as I did with but little ability to bide your time. But we must admit that in some people there is a permanent distortion of the personality. You may know a neighbour with a jealous temperament. People like that manage, usually without knowing what they are doing, to provoke their immediate environment to act in just such a way that it makes them jealous. These people are unhappy, and are uncomfortable to live with, and I would not mean that this kind of jealousy is healthy.

In the discussion there was one mother who was particularly honest in talking about herself, and the way her jealousy of her brother persisted:

MOTHER

"Well, I was an only child . . . at three my mother presented me with a baby brother. I didn't think it was very funny. I was jealous as a schoolchild, and I used to bite him, I did. . . . He never used to know that I'd done it, mind, and I never admitted I'd done it . . . but even now—I'm twenty-nine, my brother's twenty-six—and Mum will

say, 'Well, it's like this. I've just bought William so-and-so,'
and I say, 'Oh, did you?' You see? Sort of 'I don't care.'
She says, 'All right, all right, what shall I buy you?' And
she'll tell me exactly what she paid for William and make
sure that I get exactly the same. She bought him a signet
ring. . . . I know it's silly, I know it's catty, I mean, I'm married and he isn't married, but if she buys a signet ring for
him I promptly come back and say, 'Can't he afford to buy
his own?' You see? I got a birthstone ring the next week."

DWW

In people with really jealous temperaments we can be
sure that for them there was once, in their early days, a good
cause for jealousy. The unfortunate thing for really jealous
people is that they had no clear chance to be angry and jealous and aggressive at the time when this would have been
sensible and manageable. If they had had such a chance
they would probably have got through the jealous phase
and come out of it as most children do. Instead the jealousy
went right inside and the real reason for it got lost, and so
wrong reasons for jealousy are constantly being brought forward now and the claim made that they are justifiable in the
present. The way to prevent such distortion is for you to
give your small children the sort of early care which enables
them to be jealous at the appropriate moment. I suppose
that in health jealousy changes into rivalry and ambition.

[1960]

SIX

What Irks?

DWW

There are some people who are rather shocked if they find they can have other than loving feelings towards small children. If you listen to the following conversation you will find that these mothers happen to be people who are pretty certain about loving; they take it for granted, and they are not shy to talk about the seamy side of home life. These mothers were definitely asked to talk about what they felt was irksome to them, and they found no difficulty apparently in responding to the invitation. Here is the beginning:

MOTHERS

"Well, I wanted you to come here this afternoon to tell me what you find irksome about being a mother. Mrs. W., how many children have you got, first of all?"

"I have seven children, ages from twenty to three."

"Do you, in fact, find it rather an irksome job, being a mother?"

"Well, yes I do, I think, on the whole, if I'm quite truthful. I think the difficulty really in a family is the little annoying things like the constant untidiness and always chasing about to try and get them to bed—those sort of things I find irksome."

"Mrs. A.?"

"Well, I've got only two children—one a toddler and one a baby, and of course it's the poor toddler that irritates me. Like Mrs. W. it is the little things and also lack of time to cope with the children—it always seems to be a rush and my young son always wants to go and do something else when we have about two winks in which to get ready to go out."

"Mrs. S.?"

"Yes, I have two girls, one three and one just a year and I think I agree with the other two—that the time is a big thing, that there is never quite enough time to do all that I'd like to do."

"Do you mean there are other things than looking after the children that you'd like to be doing and you aren't—things for yourself?"

"Well, yes, I think there are. I do love looking after the children and—on the whole I find it's a pretty rewarding but a hurried business. I think that when I get tired it's particularly difficult. I do get tired at times. I do my best not to but it's not very easy. . . ."

"What do you think causes the tiredness among mothers? Do you think it's that you have too many jobs to do in a limited time, or is it a kind of fighting against the situation?"

"No, I think it's too many jobs to do in a limited time. At say six o'clock bedtime, one has had tea with the children, the tea things have to be washed up, the other child has to be fed and supper has to be prepared for your husband—all to be done in about an hour." (*laughter*)

DWW

Here's a good start. With several children your home can't look tidy, and it's impossible to keep a tidy mind. It's always a rush, because you have to keep an eye on the clock and all that sort of thing. And children—the smaller ones at any rate—haven't got to the age at which it can be fun to conform and to copy the grownups. The world was made for them and they act on this assumption. Then there is this matter of tiredness which is always important. When you are tired things that are usually interesting can become irksome, and if you haven't had enough sleep you are fighting a need for sleep, and this leaves less of you for the enjoyment of all the very interesting things the children are doing, which are signs every day of their development.

You will have noticed that this time I am talking about mothers and their feelings rather than about the children they are looking after. It's only too easy to idealise a mother's job. We know well that every job has its frustrations and its boring routines and its times of being the last thing anyone would choose to do. Well, why shouldn't the care of babies and children be thought of that way too? I think these mothers won't remember exactly what they felt like in a few years' time and they would be very interested to play over this recording at a time when they had reached the calm waters of a grandmotherly status.

MOTHERS

". . . all to be done in about an hour."

"We have complete chaos every night from half-past-five until half-past-seven . . . when we really don't know if we're coming or going. Things are supposed to happen at certain times but they never do because something else dreadful happens—somebody spills their milk, or something dreadful—or even—the cat gets on somebody's bed and they can't go to sleep because the cat is there or isn't there, and they come down six times to see what I'm doing, and there is complete chaos." (*laughter*)

DWW

I like that bit about the cat, which either is there or isn't there! It's not a matter of your doing things rightly or wrongly. What's wrong is just the way things are, which makes it look as if the other way round would be right, but of course it wouldn't be. Or perhaps you don't notice all the things that go well, but everything that goes wrong a little bit becomes an awful issue resulting in screams and yells.

In the next bit a mother refers to something that must be very common, the feeling that some special skill is getting rusty in her, or something that it would be fun for her to learn has to be postponed almost indefinitely.

MOTHERS

"Do you find that there are things for yourself that you would like to be doing, like writing a novel or baking a special cake or anything peculiar to yourself that the children prevent you from doing?"

"Well, I am very interested in social work and all those kinds of things. I would like to do things I have been told I could do or offered a part in even if I've not been able to because I haven't had the time, and I have found it very frustrating not to be able to do any of these things because I have to be at home."

"Yes, I did a sewing class last year which I thoroughly enjoyed, but when the second child came along I just found I couldn't get ready in time and then by about eight o'clock I thought, 'Oh dear, I really can't be bothered to go out to it.'"

"Are there things that you would like to be doing?"

"Yes, I'm very fond of sewing and that's a very irritating job when children . . . (*laughter*) . . . I really like it and I get frightfully immersed in it and let time slip by rather and that leads to trouble and I'm not a good timekeeper either. I like to forget about time very much."

"I find one very irritating thing is to have to stop whatever I'm doing in the morning and prepare a meal—a midday meal which I would get by with on something like a boiled egg, but . . . I have a husband as well so I have to . . ." (*talking together*)

DWW

Here are husbands coming in along with the children, expecting things and completely destroying any effort the wife—mother—may be making to preserve a personal interest of her own, one that demands concentration. It's just here that the wife may easily find herself wishing she were like a man, with a nice tidy job, office hours, or trade union rules and regulations protecting him from the very things that she finds irksome. I think that at this stage she can't possibly understand how it is that some men can envy women—envy them because they are at home, and because they are cluttered up with chores and in a most gorgeous mess of babies and children. So here we go back to the mess and the untidiness.

MOTHERS

"I think the untidiness I find a dreadful problem because I have domestic help and when I've gone all over the house and tidied it all up within twenty-five minutes you would think I hadn't touched it for two or three years, because it's full of toys which they must have and little bits of paper which they must cut up. I shouldn't complain about it—they must do it of course, and it's a great frustration not to make any fuss about it, but you let them do it."

"Well, I find that when mine are little, up to the age of about four, school age we'll say, going to first school, they want to be where I am, and if I'm cooking in the kitchen, well, that means they are also cooking in the kitchen, and if I'm doing things upstairs, they are also upstairs. They don't go away from me, they follow me about, which is intensely irksome, I think, at times."

DWW

So what about keeping the mess in one place?

MOTHERS

"Do you find it easier to let them roam at will anywhere in the house or do you try and confine them to their own quarters?"

"No, I have one room which I hope and pray they will not make an awful mess in, but they invariably do make an awful mess in every room in the house—they do go every-where."

"Do you think it's possible to confine them?"

"Well, I don't know if I've been lucky, but Christopher seems to realise that he is supposed to play in the nursery."

"How old?"

"Two years—over two."

"Can he see you from the nursery?"

"No, no, it's away from the kitchen, but it's a flat so we're all on the same level so he can just come along—he'll come and play in the kitchen as well. Which, of course, a lot of people think is wrong. I didn't think of putting up a barrier until it was too late. In the sitting-room and the dining-room we have old-fashioned door handles and he can't quite get his hand around them, so they, so far, have been kept tidy."

DWW

There's nothing for it; it has to be accepted that mothers with several small children do tend to live in a shoe. For the time being they don't know what to do. Perhaps as the children grow older peace returns to the fold, but perhaps not.

MOTHERS

"We have one extraordinary battle every night over the question of the dogs' dinner—who is going to give the dogs their dinner. There's a rota, you see, for giving the dogs their dinner, but there's always some reason why the person whose turn it is shouldn't do it. (*laughter*) And it will take a good twenty-five minutes when you have your dogs lined up, you see, before the dogs get any dinners at all because this frightful arguing which I—suddenly I find very irksome—the arguing that goes on in big families. Not only about dogs' dinners but when you sit down to a meal somebody will say something and before you know it there you are—everybody is shouting everybody else down because it's all a matter of principle, you see—and we've frightful arguments on all kinds of subjects."

DWW

All these examples illustrate in how many ways the care of small children can be irksome, and this is true however much the children are loved and wanted. The problem is one for the mother whose privacy is being invaded. Surely somewhere there is a little bit of herself that is sacrosanct, that can't be got at even by her own child? Shall she defend herself or surrender? The awful thing is that if the mother has something hidden away somewhere, that is exactly what the small child wants. If there is no more than a secret, then it is the secret that must be found and turned inside out. Her handbag knows all about this. Next week I would like to develop this theme of the strain on the mother.

✽   ✽   ✽

At the end of last week, after the mothers of small children had been talking about things that are irksome for mothers, I took up one idea and gave it special emphasis: the way mothers have their privacy invaded and turned inside-out. I want to develop this idea because I think it has a lot to do with what can be irksome for parents, and for mothers especially.

You will remember that these are mothers who like being married and having children, and they are fond of their children, and they wouldn't have it differently; but when they were definitely asked to refer to what annoyed them, they responded with gusto.

There will be some who will not have had the same kind of experiences. Some, at one extreme, had a worse time, got completely distracted and muddled, and had to get help. Here the muddle won, and so the mother became irritable or in some other way she was unable to go on being herself as she would like to be. Others at the other extreme will have had no feeling of disorder and invasion; they were able to keep the parlour neat and clean and somehow their infants and small children fitted into a set pattern, and there was peace most of the time. Here the mother and her essentially rigid system of rights and wrongs dominated the scene, and the infants and children had to adapt, whether ready to adapt or not. There is, of course, a lot to be said for peace and order, *if* it can be got without too much stunting of the children's spontaneity.

It is always necessary for us to remember that there are all kinds of parents and all kinds of children, and on this basis we can discuss the variations without saying that one kind is good and another kind is bad. But don't you think that extremes, one way or another, are usually signs of there being something wrong somewhere?

Often parents will say that in Victorian days it was easy, children were relegated to the nursery and nobody thought, whenever they did or didn't do something, that they were all the time building up or breaking down a child's mental health. But even in the Victorian era the vast majority of people brought up children all on the floor and round their feet, and making a mess and a noise just here, there and everywhere, and without the help of nurses with starched aprons. Every age has its customs, but I think something has stayed the same always, this awful tendency of the small child to get right into the centre where mothers keep their secrets. The question is: can a mother defend herself successfully and keep her secrets without at the same time depriving the child of an essential element—the feeling that the mother is accessible? At the beginning the child was in possession, and between possession and independence there must surely be a half-way house of accessibility.

The onlooker can easily remember that it is only for a limited time that this mother is free-house to her children. She had her secrets once and she will have them again. And she will count herself lucky that for a while she was infinitely bothered by the infinite claims of her own children.

For the mother who is right in it there is no past and no future. For her there is only the present experience of having no unexplored area, no North or South Pole but some intrepid explorer finds it, and warms it up; no Everest but a climber reaches to the summit and eats it. The bottom of her ocean is bathyscoped, and should she have one mystery, the back of the moon, then even this is reached, photographed, and reduced from mystery to scientifically proven fact. Nothing of her is sacred.

Who would be a mother? Who indeed, but the actual mother of children! And some rather special people; those children's nurses who find a way of working in with the actual parents.

You may ask, what is the use of trying to put into words what's irksome about being a mother? I think mothers are helped by being able to voice their agonies at the time that they are experiencing them. Bottled up resentment spoils the loving which is there at the back of it all. I suppose that's why we swear. A word at the right moment gathers together all the resentment and publicises it, after which we settle down to a new period of getting on with whatever we are doing. In practice I find that mothers are helped by being brought into touch with their bitter resentments. Incidentally most of them don't need help, but for the benefit of those who do need help I once wrote down a list of a dozen or so main reasons why mothers might find they hate their children.* You'll understand that I am talking about mothers who do love their children, and who are not afraid to look at their other feelings. For instance, this particular baby is not the baby the mother conceived of; not exactly the idea of a baby that she had in her mind. In a way a picture she painted might seem more her own creation than the baby who has become so real a thing in her life. The real baby certainly didn't come by magic. This actual boy or girl came by a laborious process, one which involved the mother in danger both during the pregnancy and during the birth. This actual baby that is now hers hurts her when suckling even although the process of feeding can be very satisfactory. Gradually the mother discovers that the child treats her like an unpaid servant and demands attention, and at the beginning is not concerned for her welfare. Eventually the baby bites her and it is all in love. The

*D. W. Winnicott, "Hate in the Countertransference," in *Through Paediatrics to Psycho-Analysis* (London: Hogarth, 1975; New York: Basic Books, 1958).

mother is expected to love this baby wholeheartedly at the beginning, lock, stock and barrel, the nasty bits as well as the nice bits and the mess included. Before long the baby begins to get disillusioned about the mother and shows it, refusing good food which is offered so that the mother becomes doubtful about herself. And the baby's excited love is cupboard love and after satisfaction has been obtained the mother gets thrown away like orange peel. Shall I go on with this list of reasons why a mother might hate her baby?

In these early stages the baby has no knowledge at all about what the mother is doing well, and what sacrifices she makes in order to do it well, but if things go wrong complaints appear in the form of yells. After experiencing an awful morning of screaming and temper tantrums, the mother goes out shopping with her baby and the baby smiles at a stranger who says: "Isn't he sweet!" or "Isn't she a nice friendly little creature!" The mother has a shrewd idea all the time that if she fails her baby at the start there will be a long period of paying for it, whereas if she succeeds she has no reason whatsoever to expect gratitude. You can easily think up a dozen or so reasons of your own. Probably you won't find anything worse than the one I am picking out for discussion, the way children invade your inmost reserve. If possible I would like to make some sense of this for you.

At the very beginning there is no difficulty, because the baby is in you and part of you. Although only a lodger, so to speak, the baby in the womb joins up with all the ideas of babies you ever had, and at the beginning the baby actually is the secret. The secret becomes a baby.

You have plenty of time in nine months to develop a special relationship to this phenomenon, secret turned baby, and by the time you are a few months gone you are able to identify yourself with the baby that is in you. To reach this state of affairs you have to have a rather calm state of mind, and you are immensely helped if your husband is absolutely in it with you, and is dealing with the world for both of you.

It seems to me that this special relationship to the baby comes to an end, but not at exactly the time of the birth of the baby. I think this special state of affairs lasts a few weeks after the birth, unless there are special circumstances unfortunately bringing you down to earth, like having to leave the maternity ward, or having to dismiss an unsuitable nurse, or your husband getting ill, or something.

If you are lucky and there are no awkward complications, the special state can start to end gradually. Then you start on a process of re-establishing yourself as a grown-up person in the world, and this takes several months. Your baby needs you to be able to do this, although the process brings pain for the baby. There now starts a tremendous struggle—the baby, no longer being the secret—makes a claim on all your secrets. Although fighting a losing battle your baby stakes claim after claim in a perpetual gold rush, but the gold is never enough; a new claim must be staked. And in any case you are recovering your own individual separate status, and your gold mines become ever more and more inaccessible.

You don't quite recover, however. If you did, it would mean you had finished with being a parent. And of course if you have several children the same process starts up again and again, and you are forty-five years old before you can look around and see where you yourself stand in the world.

This is a big subject that I have started up, and I only have time to say one more thing. I do believe from talking to innumerable mothers and from watching their children grow, that the mothers who come off best are the ones who can surrender at the beginning. They lose everything. What they gain is that in the course of time, they can recover, because their children gradually give over this perpetual staking of claims and are glad that their mothers are individuals in their own right, as indeed they themselves quickly become.

You perhaps know that children who are deprived of certain essential elements of home life (in fact the sort of things we've been talking about) tend to have a permanent feeling of resentment; they bear a grudge against something, but as they don't know what that something is, society has to take the strain and the children are then called antisocial.

So I feel rather hopeful about these mothers who describe their battle on behalf of the clock against the invading hordes of their children. In the end this battlefield is not strewn with corpses, but with individual children who are not deprived children, who are not problem children, or delinquent. Instead the children are adolescents, each able to stand up in his or her own right. And it's when your children exist in their own right that you can afford to do so too. You can afford to be yourself, with your secrets, which brings you back (although with a difference) to where you were before you were invaded by your children.

❀   ❀   ❀

Last week I did all the talking, and I chose one aspect of the problem of these mothers because I thought it could be important. I never forget that mothers of small children are usually tired and are often lacking sleep, but I chose to talk about the mother's loss of her privacy. This week I would like to get back to the discussion. In the extract which follows you will hear about struggles that go on between the children in a family, what might be called internecine feuds, and their effects on the mother's nerves.

MOTHERS

"I find they quarrel so much. I really do wonder why. You'd think they were bitter enemies instead of loving brothers and sisters—they fight and shout—they are, I think, very fond of each other underneath it all. If an outsider comes in they will all band together and stand up for each other, or if anybody is sick they will run down to bring home a little something, but they quarrel from morning till night and I think it gets on my nerves to come in and hear, 'You did.' 'No I didn't.' 'Yes you did.' 'Yes I shall.' 'No I shan't.' 'Yes you will.' 'I hate you.' And doors bang and they start bashing each other about you see, and I'm rushing to tear them apart. They do quarrel dreadfully."

"I suppose it's a way of working off energy—nervous and otherwise."

"I expect so, but it's very irritating."

"It's terrible on a mother's nerves. Yes, I can remember that happening too. My younger sister and I used to bicker . . . and I used to get my mother down."

"This is just wear and tear on mothers. It's nothing really big. Well, the big things I think you can always cope with them because they're rather unusual . . . it's a crisis that someone can rise to. . . . (*talking together*) . . . It's the little everyday constant sort of things, like a drip on stone, isn't it—drip, drip, drip."

DWW

Yes, drip drip drip! and to what purpose? There is a purpose, you know. Last week I said that in my opinion each child goes right in and claims whatever is there, and now I want to add that if anything is found there the children use it, and use it up. There is no quarter given, no mercy shown, no half-measures. The mother gets rough usage. Her source of energy is reached and tapped, and with boring repetition drained. Her main job is survival. Boring repetition is a thing that comes into the next bit.

MOTHERS

"We have 'good night' stories which I do find rather irksome, because I've told them every night without fail—and if ever we're going out, of course they sense it, don't they—children . . ."

"Oh, yes, they do."

"You can't cut short a line, you can't even say . . . which would normally do—it has to be done every single night if you're sick or well or dead or dying—two dreadful stories have to be read and I do think that sometimes is . . ."
(*talking together*)

"Yes, I could just take that little book and tear it up."

DWW

". . . and tear it up." There might be quite a few listening who will be glad to hear those words just once uttered. Yet the stories will go on being repeated, and accurately repeated, and children will go on needing these limited territories which they know in detail and in which there are no surprises. It's this certainty that there will be no surprises that makes for restfulness and prepares the way for a slipping over into sleep.

The next quotation from the discussion deals with the unrewarding stages, the times when a child who is developing well for one reason or another has to go back or becomes unresponsive or definitely defiant. Here a little girl deals with her jealousy of the baby by losing her own achievement and becoming like a baby.

MOTHERS

"My older daughter has been able to dress herself now for—oh, nine months, and she suddenly decided she's not going to dress herself any more. She's perfectly capable. She can't do zips and buttons up behind, but she can do the ones up in front, but she says 'No,' she's going to be a baby and she sprawls on my lap like the little one—so there we are, I now have to dress them both in the morning and undress them both at night."

"Well, I can foresee this business of letting them dress themselves. I don't have to do it yet because he isn't capable yet, but I can see that this is going to be an irritating point to me—watching him slowly putting things on the wrong way round.... (*talking together*) ... because I can't— I like to do things quickly."

DWW

This is another thing that can be irksome, adapting to each child's rhythm. By temperament some children are slower than their mothers and some quicker. It's a big problem for a mother to adapt to each child's needs in this matter of quickness and slowness. Especially irksome is the task of a quick mother adapting to a rather backward child. Yet if the child and the mother get out of touch with each other on this matter of timing, the child loses the ability to act, becomes stupid, and leaves more and more to the mother or nurse. For the child, it's just as bad when the child is quick and the mother is slow, as you will readily imagine. The mother may be slow, perhaps, because she is in a depressed mood, but the child doesn't know about reasons why, and can't allow for them. No doubt a certain amount can be done by planning, but young children tend to upset the best plans, simply because they can't see any need for looking ahead. They live in the present. In the next bit, we hear about planning:

MOTHERS

"Well, part of this lack of time is this business of organising oneself in order to go out—planning one's afternoon to fit in a feed at two o'clock and get back for a feed at six o'clock. The shopping I think is the main thing because I go down to a market about four miles away which is very cheap and it's quite a performance getting both children, one fed by bottle and one fed by spoon, both dressed and ready to go out—and one of them has a sleep anyway which makes it even later—and then rushing madly around trying to get back in time to feed the other one with the bottle again. Then there are other things like going out to tea sometimes . . . this afternoon for instance getting us organised. It takes about an hour to get the three of us ready."

"It's a terrible job."

"By the time you've got yourself ready and the other two, I mean . . ."

"Yes, the other two seem to have—they've got a bit scruffy."

"It's the planning of it—the thinking out the best times to go."

"The small examples like that are probably the most irksome of all—I think they're the most irritating, yes."

"After all, I mean, I love my two children. I don't find them irritating all the time, it's just the little things."

"Something that does annoy me a little bit is the next meal—what they're going to have—what they're all going to have."

"Do you plan meals very far ahead?"

"No, no. I'm not a planner. Something sort of—you know—as we get nearer the meal . . . (*laughter*) . . . something materialises. . . . Mind you, I shop—I do one shop a week so I have enough in the house for the following week, but when and where it's to be used, it's not decided until a fairly late hour."

"Well, I'm amazingly lucky about lunch, because Christopher's favourite meal is mince. I'm fed up with mince." (*laughter*)

"They've got a very limited taste haven't they sometimes. Makes it easy . . ."

"Yes, very easy."

DWW

A bit of hope creeping in. But a mother plans, and she does as much organising as possible, but somehow she can't bring together the needs of each child and the dictatorship of the clock, the relative distance between home and shop, and the fact of her own limited strength. In the end we return to the picture of a mother struggling to cope at one and the same time with the children's individual needs and with the world as she knows it.

MOTHERS

". . . But another great irritation is having to interrupt my household jobs—my vacuum-cleaning or something—I feel that I can get the room done in ten minutes if only I'm allowed to, but to have somebody come up behind me and 'I need to do potty'—he's sitting on the potty and you've got to be there—you've got to be there and . . ."

"Yes, you can't go away and do something else."

"And he makes it into a game." (*laughter*)

"And then something boils over on the stove, and you've left the vacuum-cleaner on because you think you'll only be a minute . . ."

"Oh, I find constant interruptions very irritating—I suddenly hear a scream from somewhere and have to put everything down whether it's cooking—floury hands and everything—and rush out to find out what's happened."

"Well, if I have floury hands I say, 'Look, you don't want me to do anything with my hands like this, do you?'"

"And that works?"

"Yes. 'I'll do it later.' I'm afraid I do that a lot, and also when we've—when irritating things crop up like 'Oh dear, we've left such and such behind,' Elizabeth says, you know, we'll be going out somewhere and she was going to take a doll, or she was going to take a shopping basket—I say, 'Oh well, you'll have to bring it next time.' It's like a dream at the moment."

DWW

There is a limit, and all the time as each child grows there is a more and more clearly defined limit to the demands that a small child has a right to make on the mother. And who shall set this limit? To some extent, the mother finds she can gradually defend herself.

MOTHERS

"Lots depends on what sort of night you had as well." (*laughter*)

"I'd had a dreadful night and I really was cross with him that day and if he showed any signs of being annoying, I'm afraid I just sort of blew up."

"And does it make him worse?"

"No, I think he senses that I've really come to the end of things and he'd better be quiet. And he surprisingly is."

DWW

But I expect in the end it's the father who has to come in and defend his wife. He has his rights too. Not only does he want to see his wife restored to an independent existence, but also he wants to be able to have his wife to himself, even if at certain times this means the exclusion of the children. So in the course of time the father puts his foot down, which brings me back to my talk of several weeks ago on "Saying 'No'." In one of those programmes I suggested that particularly when the father puts his foot down that he becomes significant for the small child, provided he has first earned the right to take a firm line by being around in a friendly sort of way.

Irksome indeed the care of small children can be, but the alternative, the regimentation of the very young child, is the most awful idea a mother can think of. So I suppose children will go on being a nuisance and mothers will go on being glad they had the chance to be the victims.

[1960]

SEVEN

Security

Whenever an attempt is made to state the basic needs of
infants and of children, we hear the words "what children
need is security." Sometimes we may feel this is sensible
and at other times we may feel doubtful. It may be asked,
what does the word *security* mean? Certainly parents who
are overprotective cause distress in their children just as
parents who can't be reliable make their children muddled
and frightened. Evidently then it is possible for parents to
give too much security, and yet we know that children do
need to feel secure. How can we sort this out?

Parents who can manage to keep a home together do in
fact provide something that is immensely important to their
children, and naturally when a home breaks up there are
casualties among the children. But if we are just simply
told that children need security, you would feel that something must be missing in this statement. Children find in
security a sort of challenge, a challenge to them to prove
that they can break out. The extreme of the idea that security is good would be that a happy place to grow up in
would be a prison. This would be absurd. Of course there

can be freedom of the spirit anywhere, even in a prison. The poet Lovelace wrote:

> *Stone walls do not a prison make,*
> *Nor iron bars a cage*

implying that there is more to be thought of than the actual fact of being held fast. But people must live freely in order to live imaginatively. Freedom is an essential element, something that brings out the best in people. Nevertheless we have to admit that there are some who can't live in freedom because they fear both themselves and the world.

To sort out these ideas, I think we must consider the developing infant, child, adolescent, adult, and trace the evolution not only of individual persons but also of what is needed of the environment by these individuals as they evolve. Certainly it is a sign of healthy growth when children begin to be able to enjoy the freedom that can increasingly be given to them. What are we aiming at in bringing up children? We hope that each child will gradually acquire a sense of security. There must build up inside each child a belief in something; not only something that is good but also something that is reliable and durable or that recovers after having been hurt or after being allowed to perish. The question is, how does this building up of a sense of security take place? What leads to this satisfactory state of affairs, in which the child has confidence in the people around and in things? What brings out the quality we call self-confidence? Is the important thing an innate or personal factor or is it moral teaching? Must there be an example that is to be copied? Is an external environmental provision necessary to produce the desired effect?

We could review the stages of emotional development through which every child must pass in order to become a healthy and eventually an adult person. This would take a long time but it could be done. In the course of this review we could talk of the innate processes of growth in the individual and the way (necessarily very complex) in which human beings become persons in their own right. Here, however, I want to refer to the environmental provision, the part we play and the part that society plays in relation to us. It is the surroundings that make it possible for each child to grow, and without adequate environmental reliability the personal growth of a child can't take place, or such growth must be distorted. And as no two children are exactly alike, we are required to adapt specifically to each child's needs. This means that whoever is caring for a child must know that child and must work on the basis of a personal living relationship with that child, not on the basis of something learnt and applied mechanically. Being reliably present and consistent to ourselves we provide the stability which is not rigid but which is alive and human, and this makes the infant feel secure. It is this in relation to which the infant can grow and which the infant can absorb and copy.

When we offer security we do two things at once. On the one hand because of our help the child is safe from the unexpected, from innumerable unwelcome intrusions and from a world that is not yet known or understood. And also, on the other hand, the child is protected by us from his or her own impulses and from the effects that these impulses might produce. I need hardly remind you that very young infants need care absolutely and can't get on on their own. They need to be held, to be moved, to be cleaned up, to be fed, and to be kept at the right temperature and to be protected from draughts and bangs. They need their impulses to be met and they need us to make sense of their spontaneity. There is not much difficulty at this early stage because in most cases each infant has a mother, and the mother at this time concerns herself almost entirely with her infant's needs. At this stage the infant is secure. When a mother succeeds in this thing that she does at the beginning the result is a child whose difficulties really do belong not to the impingements of the world but to life and to the conflict that goes with live feelings. In the most satisfactory circumstances, then, in the security of infant care that is good enough, the infant starts living a personal and individual life.

Very soon infants begin to be able to defend themselves against insecurity, but in the first weeks and months they are but feebly established as persons and so if unsupported they become distorted in their development when untoward things happen. The infant that has known security at this early stage begins to carry around an expectation that he or she won't be let down. Frustrations—well, yes, these are inevitable; but being let down,—well, no! All this is pretty straightforward.

The question we are concerned with here is, what happens when a sense of security becomes established in the child? I want to say this. There then follows one long struggle *against* security, that is to say, security that is provided in the environment. The mother, after the initial period of protection, gradually lets the world in, and the individual small child now pounces on every new opportunity for free expression and for impulsive action. This war against security and controls continues throughout childhood; yet the controls go on being necessary. The parents continue to be ready with a disciplinary framework, with the stone walls and iron bars, but insofar as they know what each child is like, and insofar as they are concerned with the evolution of their children as persons, they welcome defiance. They continue to function as custodians of the peace but they expect lawlessness and even revolution. Fortunately in most cases relief is obtained both for the children and for the parents through the life of imagination and play, and by cultural experiences. In time and in health children become able to retain a sense of security in the face of manifest insecurity, as for instance when a parent is ill or dies or when someone misbehaves or when a home for some reason or other breaks up.

Children need to go on finding out whether they still can rely on their parents, and this testing may continue till the children are themselves ready to provide secure conditions for their own children and after. Adolescents quite characteristically make tests of all security measures and of all rules and regulations and disciplines. So it usually happens that children do accept security as a basic assumption. They believe in good early mothering and fathering because they've had it. They carry with them a sense of security and this is constantly being reinforced by their tests of their parents and of their family and of their school teachers and of their friends and of all sorts of people they meet. Having found the locks and bolts securely fastened, they proceed to unlock them, and to break them open; they burst out. And again and again they burst out. Or else they curl up in bed and play blue jazz records and feel futile.

Why do adolescents especially make such tests? Don't you think it's because they're meeting frighteningly new and strong feelings in themselves, and they wish to know that the external controls are still there? But at the same time they must prove that they can break through these controls and establish themselves as themselves. Healthy children do need people to go on being in control, but the disciplines must be provided by persons who can be loved and hated, defied and depended on; mechanical controls are of no use, nor can fear be a good motive for compliance. It's always a living relationship between persons that gives the necessary elbow room which true growth needs. True growth carries the child or adolescent on to an adult sense of responsibility, especially a responsibility for the provision of secure conditions for the small children of a new generation. Isn't it possible to see all this going on in the works of creative artists of all kinds? They do something very valuable for us, because they are constantly creating new forms and breaking through these forms only to create new ones. Artists enable us to keep alive, when the experiences of real life often threaten to destroy our sense of being really alive and real in a living way. Artists of all people best remind us that the struggle between our impulses and the sense of security (both of which are vital to us) is an eternal struggle and one that goes on inside each one of us as long as our life lasts.

In health then children develop enough belief in themselves and in other people to hate external controls of all kinds; controls have changed over into self-control. In self-control the conflict has been worked through within the person in advance. So I see it this way: good conditions in the early stages lead to a sense of security, and a sense of security leads on to self-control, and when self-control is a fact, then security that is imposed is an insult.

[1960]

EIGHT

Feeling Guilty

CLAIRE RAYNER*: When my daughter was just a few weeks old, a relative of mine telephoned in quite a disguised voice and said she was an official of the NSPCC. Now oddly enough, although in the past I'd always spotted these jokes when she played them on me, this time I fell for it and I got a terrific uprush of guilty fear. I mean I was afraid, what had I done to cause this. I found this a very interesting reaction. It took me some time to get over it; in fact the whole day. I still had this nasty sick feeling inside that I'd done something I shouldn't.

DWW: Mm, I should think so. But apart from feeling guilty, isn't there here something just to do with the fact that a sudden thing had come in, just at a time when you were not really back in the world? I mean I was thinking that just before you have a baby and just afterwards, you're in rather a protected position in the world and you don't expect these sorts of things. Wouldn't something, even a big noise or anything unexpected, make you feel awful just at that time?

*Claire Rayner, who trained as a nurse, is a writer and well-known radio and television broadcaster. She is the author of many books on child care and health.

CR: Well, yes, I agree there, but this was so specifically a feeling of guilt. You know there are so many fears, aren't there? You hear a loud noise and you get one sort of fear, and you get the fear—the anticipatory fear something nasty is going to happen—you're going to the dentist and you've got that sort of fear. But this was a guilty fear. I had done something wrong and I was going to be caught out, you know; this was the way I felt. That I'd been discovered in a crime.

DWW: Yes, well, I do see what you mean, and I like the idea of discussing this with you because there's something that's interested me very much, and that is that in talking as observer and psychologist and all that sort of thing, talking to mothers, and fathers, about their children, I find that however careful one is, one tends to make them feel guilty. I've taken a lot of trouble to try and put things in such a way that it's not critical and that it's trying to explain things rather than to say this is wrong and all that. And yet people constantly come to me and say, every time you talk, or every time I read something you write, I feel so wicked; so I'm rather interested in this problem.

CR: Well, that's one sort of guilt, isn't it? Someone reads an article or a book that says you should do this and they immediately feel guilty because they haven't. But there are other thoughts. I know one young woman who I don't think had ever done any reading of articles of this sort who as soon as her baby arrived developed a cleaning compulsion. I mean she'd been an ordinary average sort of housewife before, but once the baby turned up she—she scrubbed everything that he—he came in contact with to

within an inch of its life. She changed his clothes three or
four times a day, couldn't bear it if he had a mark on him, if
he was at all dirty, and as he grew older, this extended itself. You see when he was tiny it was his pram, his cot, his
own room. Now he's beginning to crawl around and this—
this cleaning thing—has extended itself to the other rooms
that he crawls in. Her living room carpet, she scrubs it
every week, shampoos it, but this seems to me an odd sort
of thing to do, I can't help feeling that she feels guilty
about something, to behave in this way. I don't know if you
agree with me?

DWW: Well, I think that it's a rather useful sort of extreme example really, because it introduces the idea that
somebody can feel guilty without knowing it, because in
that extreme, it seems to me that most observers would be
able to tell that this mother has a fear that she's—that
some harm is going to come to the child and that she has to
do everything she can, but I don't suppose she knows that
at all. She feels simply just that she feels awful if she isn't
cleaning everything up and she probably feels awful even
when she is cleaning everything up. So I think that there
must be a lot of different ways in which we could see,
when we are looking on, that somebody is probably operat-
ing under a sense of guilt and they probably don't know it.
But still there is the other end of the problem where
there's a general latent sense of guilt which is, I think,
mainly what's interesting us.

CR: Yes I thought about this a good bit. I can't help
wondering how often it can stem from jealousy between a

mother and her child. If I can be a bore and quote my own case again. When my small daughter was born I discovered—I'd got her home when this happened—that I was jealous of her in relation to my husband. I was afraid, I think—looking back at it, I didn't realise it at the time but now I do—that she would steal some of his regard from me. I didn't feel there was room for her in our relationship then. Once I'd recognised this, this quite real jealousy, it went. As soon as I admitted it was a jealousy it just disappeared, which is interesting I think. But I wonder how many other mothers feel a jealousy. If they have a daughter, what about the discrepancy in their ages? There's so much emphasis these days in magazines and so on about women being young and beautiful, is it not possible that a woman with a little girl is suddenly made very much aware of the fact that she is no longer as young as she was, no longer as young as this child is, that her life in part is over? That here is this young thing whose life is just starting. Can she feel jealous of this? Guilty about the jealousy? Do you think that's a possibility?

DWW: Well, I think that by being very frank about yourself you are describing one of ever so many different ways in which different people, various people might feel guilty because they've had ideas about their children which they weren't expecting. In your case you said you might feel jealous because you had a little girl and you're interested in your husband's reactions to the little girl and so on; well, then, if you'd had a boy that would have been different. So somebody else has a boy but they're anxious and feeling wicked because they're surprised to find that they didn't want a boy, or for some reason or another they didn't start off loving the baby as they thought they ought to. Everybody's got a pre-conceived notion of some sort of ideal state in which everything goes well and mothers and babies just love each other, and so I think that what you're drawing attention to is just one example of a whole group of reasons why any particular mother might have an unexpected emotion about her baby and feel guilty, thinking that she oughtn't to have it. And for instance it might be that she found she loved her baby perfectly naturally and this made her feel awful because she didn't feel that her mother had loved her in the same way, and then she felt she was . . . presenting her mother with an example. I mean I remember seeing a little girl sitting on the floor being awfully nice to a doll and one could tell that she was telling her mother what a rotten mother she thought her mother was to her just at that moment. I feel that in other words there's a tremendous variation of different kinds of reasons why various people can have unexpected feelings and emotions about their newborn baby. (*CR*: Yes.) But I still think there are some rather more inherent things which must be absolutely universal, if we could only get at them.

CR: Yes, you know I was just remembering when I was a pupil midwife I noticed that so often the mother's first question about the baby was not "What is it?" but "Is it all right?", "Is it normal?" I was interested in this then; I'm far more interested in it now. I can't help wondering why a mother should be afraid that there should be something wrong with the baby, it's a very common fear, isn't it? That you're going to produce a (*DWW*: Yes . . .) monster or something that has something wrong with it.

DWW: I think it's not only common but it's rather normal, you see. I mean there are some people—of course there are all kinds of people, there have to be and it's a good thing—but some people really separate off the having of babies from the rest of their lives to a remarkable degree. But one can't say it's necessarily normal to do so. With most people—if they have children—there's the whole fantasy of having children joined up with just actually having one. There's the whole fantasy which would have turned up in their playing at fathers and mothers when they were children, and in their ideas. There's a very variable amount of love and hate and . . . aggression mixed up with kindness and everything in it all, and so it seems to me that there is something inherent that we could find in absolutely everybody really. When they have a baby they can understand perfectly well with their minds where the baby came from, but still in their fantasies their baby is something they produced and they don't feel that they could have produced something perfect. And they're right. I mean if they tried to paint a painting, or to produce any other kind of work of art or even to cook a dinner, they can't be certain that the thing's going to be absolutely perfect. And yet they can produce a perfect baby.

CR: Would this mean then that when the mother asks this question and the answer is that the baby is normal, it's all right, perfectly normal, that her guilt, the guilt that prompted this question is gone—it's washed away?

DWW: Yes, that's what I mean really, that then the baby returns to being a baby and all the fantasies are fantasies. But if on the other hand there's just something doubtful about the baby, or the nurse even just says it's all right, only delays a little while, the mother then has time just to join up all the fantasies and the fears and the doubts with her idea of the baby and fails to get the full reassurance. And if there's really something wrong, then she has to deal with a very bad period in which she feels responsible for that, because she's had this tie-up with the idea of the baby with the actual pregnancy. (*CR*: Yes.) With the baby inside her. Two quite separate things really but they so easily don't get separated out if the baby doesn't turn out to be quite normal.

CR: Yes, I see.

DWW: And I'd say on the other hand that if the baby turns out to be quite normal, then the baby isn't as good as one of the fantasies that she had about the baby.

CR: Yes. I can't help wondering though if these feelings of guilt are so common. They must have a certain value. Guilt in itself isn't a bad thing, is it? Would it not encourage a mother's sense of responsibility towards her child in a way?

DWW: Yes. Well I think it's awfully like—if you take cooking. If somebody really had no feelings at all of doubt I don't think they'd be very interesting cooks really. The thing is that before a party for instance nearly everybody feels a bit worked up because a thing might go wrong, and of course they probably put on too much food in case there isn't enough and all that sort of thing; all these things are practically universal. But the fact is that people come to the party and enjoy it and then they eat up—even the amount that's too much. It seems to me that what you're saying is that it's really necessary for people to doubt themselves in order to feel fully responsible.

CR: Yes, yes I feel this. If you didn't feel guilty a bit about your child, you wouldn't want to protect him quite so much, would you? I mean if you just felt that everything was going to be all right and normal all the time and nothing could possibly go wrong, and the child suddenly shot a temperature, you'd say, "Oh well, nothing can go wrong; why bother? Why go to the doctor? There's no need, nothing can possibly go wrong this way..."

DWW: Yes, from my point of view it's a very practical matter because I spend a lot of my time seeing mothers who bring their children to hospital, and I feel that they come to me worried about their children, they're worried in terms of their child, and if they weren't, they wouldn't notice when the child was ill. (*CR*: Yes.) They often come when the child's quite well. A mother might say to me that the child fell yesterday and hurt his head, and "I'm just— I'm not quite sure whether he's as well as he was and is it all right?" Well, that's quite right that she should come, and my job is probably to say, "Yes, I've examined the child and the child's all right." And then I feel I'm dealing with the mother's sense of guilt about her child, which is all right—it stops once she's done her bit, she's had the thing checked up; or perhaps if she didn't have to come to the doctor she could just watch and think and see that things are all right after all. But it is the sense of guilt that makes her sensitive I think (*CR*: Yes), and have doubt about herself. Because I do find that there are parents who haven't got this capacity for a sense of guilt and who don't even notice when their children are ill.

CR: Yes, it must be rather pleasant, if I can put it that way, for the child. I mean for a little child the world and its responsibilities are enormous, overwhelming, aren't they? And a mother who is willing to accept to herself the blame for the things that happen, to blame herself and protect him in this way, it must be very pleasant for the child; mother's guilt becomes a cushion, doesn't it? Against the world at large.

DW: Yes. I think on the whole if you could choose your parents, which of course is one thing we can't do, we would rather have a mother who felt a sense of guilt—at any rate who felt responsible, and felt that if things went wrong it was probably her fault—we'd rather have that than a mother who immediately turned to an outside thing to explain everything, and said it was due to the thunderstorm last night or some quite outside phenomenon and didn't take responsibility for anything. I think of the two, certainly of the two extremes, we'd rather have the mother who felt very responsible.

[1961]

NINE

The Development of a Child's Sense of Right and Wrong

Some people think that ideas of right and wrong grow in the child like walking and talking, though some people think you have to implant them. My own view is that there is room for something in between these two extremes, there's room for the idea that the sense of good and bad, like much else, comes naturally to each infant and child, provided certain conditions of environmental care can be taken for granted. These essential conditions can't be described in a few words, but in the main it is this; that the environment should be predictable and at first highly adapted to the infant's needs. Most infants and small children do in fact get these essentials.

I do want to just say that the basis of morality is the baby's fundamental experience of being his or her own true self, of going on being; reacting to the unpredictable breaks up this going on being, and interferes with the development of a self. But this is going back too far for this discussion. I must go on to the next phase in development.

As each infant begins to collect a vast experience of going on being in his or her own sweet way and to feel that a self exists, a self that could be independent of the mother, then fears begin to dominate the scene. These fears are primitive in nature, and are based on the infant's expectation of crude retaliations. The infant gets excited, with aggressive or destructive impulses or ideas, showing as screaming or wanting to bite, and immediately the world feels to be full of biting mouths and hostile teeth and claws and all kinds of threats. In this way the infant's world would be a terrifying place were it not for the mother's general protective role which hides these very great fears that belong to the infant's early experience of living. The mother (and I'm not forgetting the father) alters the quality of the small child's fears by being a human being. Gradually she becomes recognised, by the infant, as a human being. So instead of a world of magical retaliations the infant acquires a mother who understands, and who reacts to the infant's impulses. But the mother can be hurt or become angry. When I put it this way, you will see immediately that it makes an immense difference to the infant if the retaliatory forces become humanised. For one thing, the mother knows the difference between actual destruction, and the intention to destroy. She says "Ow!" when she gets bitten. But she is not disturbed at all by recognising that the baby wants to eat her. In fact, she feels that this is a compliment, the only way the baby can show excited love. And of course, she is not so easy to eat. She says "Ow!" but that only means that she felt some pain. A baby can hurt the breast, and especially so if teeth unfortunately appear early. But mothers do survive, and babies have a chance to gain reassurance from her survival. Moreover, you do give babies something hard, don't you, something which has good survival value, like a rattle or a bone ring? Because you know that it is a relief for the baby to be able to bite all out, on to something.

In these ways, the infant has a chance to develop the use of fantasy alongside actual impulsive action, and this important step results from the mother's consistent attitude and general reliability. Also this environmental reliability provides a setting in which the next movement forward in development can take place. This next stage is one that depends on the contribution that the infant can make to the parents' happiness. The mother is there at the right moment, and she will receive the impulsive gestures that the infant makes towards her, and which mean so much to her, because they really are a part of the infant and not just reactions. There is the reactive smile that means little or nothing, but there is also the smile that eventually turns up that means that the infant feels loving, and feels loving at that moment towards the mother. Later, the infant splashes her in the bath or pulls her hair or bites the lobes of her ear or gives her a hug, and all that sort of thing. Or the infant produces an excretion in a special way that implies that the excretion has gift meaning. And that it has value. The mother feels immensely built-up by these tiny things if they are spontaneous. On account of this, the infant is able to make a new development and integration, to accept in a new and a fuller way responsibility for all the nastiness and destructiveness felt in the moments of excitement—that is to say in the experience of the instincts.

The most important instinct for the infant is that roused in feeding, and this becomes joined up with the fact of loving and liking, with affectionate play. And the fantasies of eating the mother and father become all mixed in with the reality of eating which is displaced onto the eating of food. The infant is able to start to accept full responsibility for all this ruthless destruction because of knowing about the gestures which also turn up and which indicate an impulse to give, and also because of knowing from experience that the mother will be there at the moment at which true loving impulses appear. In this way, there becomes a measure of control over what feels good and what feels bad, and so by a complex process and because of growing powers that make the infant able to hold together various experiences—what we call integration—the infant gradually becomes able to tolerate feeling anxious about the destructive elements in the instinctual experiences, knowing that there will be opportunity for repairing and rebuilding. We give this toleration of anxiety a name. We call it a sense of guilt. We can see the sense of guilt developing along with the establishment of the infant's confidence in the reliability of the environment, and we also see the capacity for a sense of guilt disappearing, along with the loss of confidence and the reliability of the environment, as when a mother has to be away from her infant, or when she is ill or perhaps just preoccupied.

Once the infant has begun to be able to have guilt feelings, that is to say to relate constructive behaviour with anxiety about destruction, then the infant is in the position to sort out what feels to be good and what feels to be bad. It is not a direct take-over from the parents' moral sense, but a new moral sense, starting up as it should in the case of each new individual. The feeling that something is right certainly links up with the infant's idea of the mother's or the parents' expectations, but more deeply rooted is the meaning of good and bad that is linked with this sense of guilt—the balance between anxiety about the destructive impulses and the capacity and opportunity for mending and for building. What lessens the guilt feelings feels good for the infant, and what increases the guilt feelings feels bad. In fact, the innate morality of the infant, as it develops out of crude fears, is much more fierce than the morality of the mother and father. Only what is true and real counts for the infant. You have quite a job teaching your child to say "Ta!" out of good manners and not from gratitude.

You will see that according to the theory I use in my work, you are making it possible for your infant to develop a sense of right and wrong by your being a reliable person in this formative early phase of your infant's living experiences. Insofar as each child has found his or her own guilt sense, so far, and only so far, does it make sense for you to introduce your ideas of good and bad.

If you can't succeed with your infant in this way (and you will be better with one infant than with another) you'll have to make the best of being a strict human being, though you know that better things could be happening in the infant's natural development process. If you fail altogether, then you must try to implant ideas of right and wrong by teaching and by drill. But this is a substitute for the real thing, and is an admission of failure, and you will hate it; and in any case this method only works as long as you, or someone acting for you, are there to enforce your will. On the other hand, if you can start your infant off so that through your reliability he or she develops a personal sense of right and wrong in place of crude and primitive fears of retaliation, then you will find later you can reinforce the child's ideas, and enrich these ideas by your own. For as children grow they like to copy their parents, or to defy them, which is just as good in the end.

[1962]

TEN

Now They Are Five

In a very recent court case a learned judge is reported to have said, in reference to the case of a child of nearly five whose parents had split up: "Children of that age are notoriously resilient." I have no wish to criticize the judgment given in this case, but it is open to us to discuss the question: Are children of five years notoriously resilient? Resilience, it would seem to me, comes only with growth and maturity, and we may hold the view that there is no time in the development of a child at which it could be said that the child is resilient. Resilience would imply that we could expect compliance on the part of the child without danger to the growth of the child's personality and the establishment of the child's character.

It might indeed be argued that there are some special features of this five-year stage which would make you especially careful not to relax your watch on environmental reliability. Tonight I'm trying to look at these special features.

You watch your children grow, and you are astonished. It's all so slow, and yet at the same time it all happens in a flash. That's the funny thing about it. A few weeks ago you had a baby. And then he was a toddler, and today he's five, and tomorrow he will be at school—or she, whichever applies. And in a few weeks he will have practically started going to work.

There is a contradiction here which is interesting. The time passed both slowly and quickly. Or, I could say, when you were feeling things from the point of view of your child time practically stood still. Or it started off still, and only gradually began to move. The idea of infinity comes from the memory traces in each one of us in our infancy before time started. But when you jump across to having your own grown-up experiences, you realise that five years is almost nothing.

This has a curious effect on the relationship between what you remember and what the child remembers. You yourself remember clearly what happened a month ago, and now suddenly you find your five-year-old is not remembering his aunt's visit or the arrival of the new puppy. He remembers some things, even early things, especially if they have been talked about, and he uses the family saga which he learns almost as if it were about someone else, or as if it referred to characters in a book. He has become more aware of himself and of the present time, and along with this he has come to forget.

He now has a past, and in his mind a hint of half-forgotten things. His teddy bear is at the back of the bottom drawer, or he has forgotten how important it once was, except when he suddenly feels a need for it again.

We could say that he is emerging from an enclosure; the walls of the enclosure began to have gaps, and the fences became uneven in thickness; and lo and behold, he's outside. It's not easy for him to get back inside again or to feel he's back inside, except if he's tired or ill, when you re-assemble this enclosure for his benefit.

The enclosure was provided by you, his mother and father, and by the family, and by the house and the courtyard, and by the familiar sights and noises and smells. It also belongs to his own stage of immaturity and to his reliance on your reliability, and to the subjective nature of the infant world. This enclosure was a natural development from your arms that you put round him when he was an infant. You adapted in an intimate way to your infant's needs, and then you gradually de-adapted, according to the rate at which he became able to enjoy meeting the unexpected and the new. So, since children are not really like each other much, you find you've made an enclosure in which each child lives, one for each child; and it's out of this enclosure that your son or daughter now emerges—ready for a different kind of group, a new kind of enclosure, at least for a few hours a day. In other words, your child will go to school.

Wordsworth referred to this change in his "Ode on the Intimations of Immortality":

> *Heaven lies about us in our infancy,*
> *Shades of the prison-house begin to close*
> *Upon the growing boy . . .*

Here surely, the poet felt the child's consciousness of the new enclosure, in contrast with the baby's unawareness of dependence.

Of course, you've already started up the process by using a nursery school if a very good one happens to be near where you live. In a good nursery school a small group of toddlers can be given opportunity for play, and can be provided with suitable toys and perhaps a better floor than you yourself own, and someone is always present to supervise your child's first experiments in social life, such as bashing the next child on the head with a spade.

But the nursery school is not much unlike home, it's still a specialised provision. The school we are now considering is different. The primary school may be good or not so good, but it will not be adaptive like the nursery school, not specialised except perhaps at the very beginning. In other words, your child will have to do the adapting, will have to fit in with what is expected of the pupils at the school. I do hope he's ready for this because if he is there is a great deal to be got out of the new experience.

You've given a lot of thought to the management of this big change in your child's life. You've already talked about school, and the child has played at schools and has looked forward to the idea of experiencing an extension of the bit of teaching you and others have already put in.

Difficulties do arise at this stage because environmental changes have to be fitted onto changes that are happening in the child because of growth. I've had quite a lot to do with difficulties of children at this age, and I would say this, that in the vast majority of cases of difficulty there is no deep-seated trouble at all, no real illness. The strain has to do with the need for one child to be quick, for another to be slow. A few months make a lot of difference. You may feel that your child whose birthday is in November is champing the bit waiting to be admitted, whereas your child whose birthday is in August gets packed off to school a month or two early. In any case, one child eagerly goes on to the deeper waters, while another tends to lie shivering on the brink and fears to launch away. And by the way, some of the brave pushers-on suddenly shrink back after putting a toe in and go back inside you and refuse to re-emerge from the enclosure for days or weeks or longer. You get to know what sort of a child you have, and so you talk to the school teachers, who are quite used to all this, and they just wait, and play the fish on a long line. The thing is to understand that coming out of the enclosure is very exciting and very frightening; and that once out, it's awful for the child not being able to get back, and that life is a long series of coming out of enclosures and taking new risks and meeting new and exciting challenges.

Some children have personal difficulties that make them unable to take new steps, and you may need help if the passing of time does not cure, or if you have other indications that a particular child is ill.

But there may be something wrong with you, the perfectly good mother, when your child shrinks back. If this can be so then I think you would not wish me to leave it out. I'll tell you what I mean.

Some mothers operate in two layers. At one layer (shall I call it the top layer?) they only want one thing, they want their child to grow up, to get out of enclosure, to go to school, to meet the world. At another layer, deeper I suppose, and not really conscious, they cannot conceive of letting their child go. In this deeper layer where logic is not very important the mother cannot give up this most precious thing, her maternal function—she feels she is maternal more easily when her baby is dependent on her than when, by growth, he comes to enjoy being separate and independent and defiant.

The child senses this only too easily. Although happy at school, he comes panting home, he screams rather than go into the school door each morning. He's sorry for you because he knows you can't stand losing him, and that you haven't got it in you to turn him out because of your nature. It's easier for him if you can be glad to be rid of him, and glad to have him back.

You see, a lot of people, including the best, are a bit depressed part of the time or almost all the time. They have a vague sense of guilt about something and they worry about their responsibilities. The liveliness of the child in the home has been a perpetual tonic. Always the child's noises, even his cries, have been a sign of life, and have just given the right reassurance. For depressed people all the time feel they may have let something die, something precious and essential. The time comes when their child is due to go to school and then the mother fears the emptiness of her home and of herself, the threat of a sense of internal personal failure which may drive her to find an alternative preoccupation. When the child comes back from school, if a new preoccupation has come about, there will be no place for him, or he'll have to fight his way back into the mother's centre. This fighting his way back becomes more important to him than school.

The common result is that the child becomes a case of school refusal. All the time he's longing to be at school, and his mother longs for him to be just like other children.

I knew a boy who at this stage developed a passion for joining things together with string. He was always tying the cushions to the mantelpiece and the chairs to the tables, so that it was precarious moving about in the house at all. He was very fond of his mother, but always uncertain of getting back to her centre because she quickly became depressed when he left her, and in no time she had replaced him with something else she was worried about or doubtful about.

If you're a bit like this you may perhaps be helped by understanding that these things often happen. You may be glad that your child is sensitive to his mother's and other people's feelings, but sorry that your unexpressed and even unconscious anxiety should make the child sorry for you. He's unable to get out of the enclosure.

You may have had an experience of this difficulty he's in at an earlier date. You may, for instance, have found it difficult to wean him. You may have come to recognise a pattern in his reluctance to take any new step, or to explore the unknown. At each of these stages you were under threat of losing your child's dependence on you. You were in the process of acquiring a child with independence and a personal slant on life, and although you could see the advantages to be gained by this you couldn't get the necessary release of feeling. There's a very close relationship between this vaguely depressive state of mind—this preoccupation with undefined anxieties—and the capacity of a woman to give a child her full attention. I can't really talk about one without referring to the other. Most women live, I suppose, just on the borderline.

Mothers have all sorts of agonies to go through, and it's rather good when the babies and the children don't have to get caught up in them. They have plenty of agonies of their own. Actually they rather like having their own agonies, just as they like new skills and a widening vision, and happiness.

What is this that Wordsworth calls the "Shades of the prison-house"? In my language it's the changeover from the small child's living in a subjective world to the older child's living in a world of shared reality. One infant starts off in magical control of the environment—if you give good enough care—and creates the world anew, even you and the door-knob. By the age of five the child has become able to perceive you more as you are, to acknowledge a world of door-knobs and other objects that existed before his conception, and to recognise the fact of dependence just at the time when he's becoming truly independent. It's all a matter of timing, and I believe you are managing it beautifully. Somehow or other people usually do. There are plenty of other ways in which life can affect your child at this age. I mentioned the child's teddy bear. Your child may well be addicted to some special object. This special object that was once a blanket or a napkin or one of your scarves or a rag doll first became important for him or her before or after the first birthday, and especially at times of transition, as from waking to sleeping life. It's immensely important; it gets treated abominably; it even smells. You are lucky that the child uses this object and not you yourself, or the lobe of your ear, or your hair.

This object joins the child to external or shared reality. It's a part both of the child and of you, the mother. One of your children with such an object has no use for it in the day, but another takes it everywhere. At five the need for this thing may not have ceased, but many other things can take its place—the child looks at comics, has a great variety of toys, both hard and soft, and there is the whole cultural life waiting to enrich the child's experience of living. But you may have trouble when the child goes to school, and you will need the teacher to go slow, and not to ban this object absolutely from the classroom just at first. This problem nearly always resolves itself within a few weeks.

I would say that the child is taking to school a bit of the relationship to you that dates right back to infantile dependence, and to early infancy, to the time when he was only beginning to recognise you and the world as separate from the self.

If the anxieties about going to school resolve themselves then the boy will be able to give up taking this object along with him, and instead will have a truck or an engine along with the string and liquorice in his pockets, and the girl will somehow manage by screwing up her handkerchief, or perhaps she'll have a secret baby in a matchbox. In any case children can always suck their thumbs or bite their nails if hard put to it. As they gain confidence they usually give up these things. You learn to expect children to show anxiety about all moves away from being part and parcel of you and of home, moves towards citizenship of the wide, wide world. And anxiety may show as a return to infantile patterns which mercifully remain to provide reassurance. These patterns become a sort of built-in psychotherapy which retains its effectiveness because you are alive and available, and because you are all the time providing a link between the present and the child's infancy experiences of which their infantile patterns are relics.

One other thing. Children tend to feel disloyal if they enjoy school and if they enjoy forgetting you for a few hours.

So they vaguely feel anxious as they get near home, or they delay their return without knowing why. If you have reason to be angry with your child please don't choose the moment of his or her return from school to express it. You too may be annoyed that you were forgotten, so look out for your own reactions to the new developments. It would be better not to be cross about that ink on the tablecloth until you and the child have re-established contact.

These things present no great difficulty if you know what's happening. Growing up is not all honey for the child, and for the mother it's often bitter aloes.

[1962]

ELEVEN

The Building Up of Trust

It should be easy to write about stress that belongs to the early ages, simply because everyone knows that very young children need continuous and reliable care, else they do not develop properly. At the next stage of individual development we expect children to have gathered into themselves innumerable samples of good care, and they go forward with a measure of belief, belief in people and in the world, so that it takes quite a big thing to knock them sideways. At the earlier age, however, this belief in things and this trust in people are in process of being built up.

This is the main thing that we notice about the very young, that although they trust us their faith can easily be shattered. For this reason we are especially careful to be reliable in essentials.

It will be understood that we do not do this by deliberate effort or by the study of books or by listening to lectures, but we do it because little children draw the best out of us, so that for a while we behave quite well. We do not even quarrel in public—that is to say, in front of the children, and we allow ourselves to seem to be drawn together by the very fact of the children's existence.

Some people are too much taken up with managing their own lives and their own difficult temperaments, so that they cannot do for the children what the children need, but children can understand a great deal so long as a home exists, and the parents are seen together, and if there is warmth even in a cold climate, and food that can be expected and enjoyed, and an absence of the sudden unpredictable noise that hurts physically and cannot be explained away. With physical conditions that can be known and, so to speak, caught hold of, children can stand some strain in the relationship between the parents, since it is, for them, a good thing that at any rate the parents are there, are alive, and have feelings. At the same time it is true that the growth of young children is more easily accomplished if they have the parents in an easy relationship the one with the other. Indeed it is the interpersonal world of the parents that is symbolised for the child by the stability of the house and the liveliness of the street, and not nearly so true the other way round, that the house and the street find symbolism in the parents' relationship with each other.

Not Idealism

I must be careful. So easily in describing what very young children need I can seem to be wanting parents to be selfless angels, and expecting the world to be ideal, like a suburban garden in summer with father cutting the grass, and mother preparing the Sunday dinner, and the dog barking at an alien dog over the garden fence. Of children, even of babies, it can be said that they do not do well on mechanical perfection. They need human beings around them who both succeed and fail.

I like to use the words "good enough." Good enough parents can be used by babies and young children, and good enough means you and me. In order to be consistent, and so to be predictable for our children, we must be *ourselves*. If we are ourselves our children can get to know us. Certainly if we are acting a part we shall be found out when we get caught without our make-up.

Danger of Teaching

My problem is to find a way of giving instruction without instructing. There is a limit to the value of being taught. Indeed it is important for parents who start looking into books for advice that they know that they do not have to know everything. Most of what goes on in the developing individual baby or child happens whether you understand it or not, simply because the child has an inherited tendency towards development. No-one has to make a child hungry, angry, happy, sad, affectionate, good or naughty. These things just happen. You have already finished that part of your responsibility and have laid down the details of your child's inherited tendencies when you chose your partner, and when the one spermatozoon penetrated the one egg. At that fateful moment the book on heredity was closed, and things started to work themselves out in terms of the body and mind and personality and character of your child. This is a matter of physiology and anatomy. The way these things work themselves out is extremely complicated, and if you wish to do so you can spend your life on an interesting research project connected with human development; such work will not, however, help you with your own child, who needs you indeed.

What to Know

What is it, then, that parents can usefully know? I would suggest that there are two main things to know, one of which has to do with the process of growth, which belongs to the child, and the other has to do with the environmental provision, which is very much your responsibility.

The Process of Growth

Once it has been pointed out to you it is surely quite obvious that your baby has a tendency to live and breathe and to eat and drink, and to grow. You will be wise if you assume these matters to be true from the very beginning.

It helps a lot to know that you do not have to make your baby into a child, to make your child grow, to make your growing child good or clean, to make your good child generous, to make your generous child clever at choosing the right presents for the right people.

If you stand back and watch you soon see the developmental process at work, and you get a sense of relief. You have started up something that has its own built-in dynamo. You will be looking for the brakes.

Every comment I make must be modified by the other observation, which is that no two children are alike, so that you may find yourself bothered by one child's lifelessness and by another child's dynamism. But the main principle holds in all cases, that it is the child's own developmental processes that make the changes you are looking for.

So the first useful principle has to do with the innate tendencies that belong to each young child.

The Environment

The second useful principle has to do with your special place as the environment and as the provider of environment. No-one has to prove to you that a baby needs gentle handling and warmth after being born. You know it to be true. If someone doubts this it is for him or her to prove that what you know is wrong.

After all, you have been a baby yourself, and you have memories to guide you, apart from all you may have learned when watching and participating in the care of babies.

The environment you provide is primarily yourself, your person, your nature, your distinguishing features that help you to know you are yourself. This includes of course all that you collect around yourself, your aroma, the atmosphere that goes with you, and it includes the man who will turn out to be the baby's father, and it may include other children if you have them, as well as grandparents and aunts and uncles. In other words, I am doing no more than describe the family as the baby gradually discovers it, including the features of the home that make your home not quite like any other home.

Interaction

So here there are two distinct things, the inborn tendencies of the baby, and the home that you provide. Life consists in the interaction of these two things. At first the interacting goes on under your very nose, and later it goes on outside the area of your immediate surroundings—at school, or in friendships, or away at a holiday camp, and of course *within* the mind or in the personal living of your boy or girl.

You could if you wished spend your time comparing your child's behaviour with some standard you have set up, based on your own family pattern, or the pattern handed out to you by someone you admired. But you may get a much richer and a much more profitable experience by comparing the child's personal struggle towards independence with the dependence which you made possible because your child had trust in you and in the general set-up of your home.

Two Kinds of Stress

I have outlined the child's development in this way in order to simplify my task of describing stress. It is possible to say that stress comes from one of two directions; although in practice we must expect to find mixtures.

The Internal Process
The first has to do with the fact that the developmental process in the human individual is extremely complicated,

and things can go wrong from within. This is what psycho-analysis is all about. There is no need whatever for parents or those who care for young children to know what are the strains and stresses which are inherent in the establishment of the individual personality and character and the gradual ability of the baby and child to make a relationship to the family and to the community, to become part of society without too great a loss of personal impulse and creativity.

Parents and others who have to do with children may find these to be matters of extreme interest; but the important thing is to be able to get there imaginatively rather than to be able to understand.

Your child playing under the table stands up and the table hits his head. He rushes to you and prepares for a good cry. You make appropriate noises and put your hand where the head got hurt, and perhaps you mend it with a kiss. After a few minutes all is well, and play under the table is resumed. What would have been the gain if you had been able to write a thesis on various aspects of this event?

1. This is the way children learn while they are playing. They must look before they leap. . . .

2. The table did not really hit the child's head, but at that age the first assumption will be of that kind, and one child is more likely than another to cling on to the "persecution" theory of trauma; this has to do with a difficulty in accepting the fact of one's own aggression, and perhaps with rage that became lost because of its painfulness as an experience for a baby or small child

who is not yet sure of keeping integrated when powerful
emotion is roused. . . .

3. Would this be a good moment for giving a lecture: "You
   see, if you move about like that without thinking you
   will hurt yourself, and one day. . . ."

No, I think it is better when the whole matter is sealed
off with a healing kiss, simply because you know what you
would be feeling like if you were that little child who has
been hit on the head by a nasty hard vindictive table. This
is called empathy and if you have not got it you cannot
learn it anywhere.

But of course, you might be a lonely person, and this
bang on the head could become a heaven-sent chance for
you to make contact with someone, so you kiss and hug,
and put the child to lie down, and you become sentimental;
perhaps you call in the doctor first to make sure there has
been no internal damage!

In this case the child has triggered off something in you
that has to do with your own problems, and for the child the
result is bewilderment. This is outside the child's understanding, and in looking at the episode we have got away
from the inherent processes in the child's living and developing. Lucky is the child who, on the whole, is left free to
get on with experiencing day by day the new things that
come within his or her ever-increasing capacity.

A great deal happens in the dark interstices of your aspidistra, if you have one, and you may be completely ignorant of biology; yet you may be famous in your street for your
aspidistra and its clean green leaves, with no brown edges.

There is no more fascinating study than that of the way a baby becomes a child and an adolescent and an adult, but a study of what is known is not part of what children need of their parents. Perhaps for teachers and those who are rather more detached from the child than parents are in everyday living experiences there is more to be said for a study of what is known and what is not known of the developmental processes. Certainly those who have care of the abnormal and those who set out to do treatment of children who are ill in terms of emotional development and in terms of personality and character, these persons do need to make a deep study of this very subject.

It is tempting to start describing the difficulties that are inherent. Let two examples suffice. One is the universal problem of ambivalence, loving and hating the same person or thing at one and the same time. Another is the experience that each child must go through to a greater or lesser extent of feeling at one with the instinctual drives as they manifest themselves in the bodily organs, or alternatively feeling more at home with the sex opposite to that of the child's body.

There are many other conflicts that we see our children suffering from and trying to solve, and we know that many children become ill because they cannot find a work solution. But it is not the job of the parent to turn psycho-therapist.

The Environmental Provision

Contrasting with the workings of the internal process in the child is the environmental provision. This is you, and it is me, and it is the school and it is society, and here we become interested in a new way because we are responsible.

For babies and young children the environmental provision either gives a chance for the internal process of growth to take place or else it prevents this very thing.

The key word could be "predictability." Parents, and especially the mother at the start, are taking a lot of trouble to shield the child from that which is unpredictable.

It will be seen that at a quick or slow pace this or that child is becoming able to put two and two together and to defeat unpredictability. There is an amazing variation here, according to the small child's capacity to defeat unpredictability. But there remains the need for mother. An aeroplane flies low overhead. This can be hurtful even to an adult. No explanation is valuable for the child. What is valuable is that you hold the child close to yourself, and the child uses the fact that you are not scared beyond recovery, and is soon off and away, playing again. Had you not been there the child could have been hurt beyond repair.

This is a crude example, but I am showing that by this way of looking at child care, stress can be described in terms of failure of environmental provision, just where reliability is needed.

It is the same thing when a mother must leave a little child in a hospital for a few days, as has been emphasized by Bowlby, and also by James and Joyce Robertson in their poignant film "A Two-Year-Old Goes to Hospital." By this age the child has really come to know the mother as a person, and it is herself that he must have, not just her care and protection. Stress at this age comes from the fact that the mother is absent over a period of time that is longer than that over which the child can keep alive the mental image of the mother, or can feel her live presence in the imaginative world of dream and play, sometimes called "inner psychic reality." Doctors and nurses are busy doing their job of body-care, and they often do not know or have no time to consider the fact that as a result of too long a separation a child's personality can be altered completely through environmental interference, and the basis can be laid down for a character disorder that we cannot mend.

It is always the same: there was good enough environmental provision in terms of predictability, according to the child's ability to predict, and then there was an unreliability that automatically broke up the continuity of the child's developmental process. After this the child has a gap in the line between now and the roots of the past. There has to be a new start. Too many of these new starts result in a failure in the child of the feeling *I am, this is me, I exist, it is I who love and hate, it is me that people see and that I see in mother's face when she comes, or in the mirror.* Growth processes become distorted because the child's integrity has broken up.

It happens that a large proportion of children, especially of the unsophisticated and the uneducated of the world, do in fact go through early childhood without having experienced this break in the continuity of life that is so disastrous. Such children have had the opportunity to develop (at any rate in the early stages) according to their own inborn tendencies towards development. They are the privileged ones.

Unfortunately a proportion of children, especially in sophisticated cultures, do have to carry round with them for life some degree of distortion of personal development caused by environmental unpredictability and the intrusion of the unpredictable, and they lose a clear sense of *I am, I am me, I exist here and now, on this basis I can enter into the lives of others, and without a sense of threat to my own basis for being myself.*

Study of Environmental Factors

I rather tended to pour cold water over the idea that parents should study the developmental processes inherent in individual growth, and based on hereditary tendencies. It is not so clear to me that a study of the environmental provision is useless. Surely, if mothers know that what they do is vitally important for their babies and small children they will be in a stronger position to fight for their rights when it is lightly suggested that mothers and babies, or mothers and young children, should be parted. This so often means that the baby is to be cared for impersonally.

The world has much to learn in this respect, especially doctors and nurses who are primarily concerned with health and disease in bodily terms. Mothers and fathers must fight their own cause here, because no-one else will fight for them. No-one else really minds as the parents mind.

This brings me to the last point, which is that even this matter of environmental provision, reliability, adaptation to infant needs, does not need to be learnt. There is something about having a baby (even preparing for adopting a baby) that alters the parents. They become orientated to the special task. I wanted to give it a name so I called it "primary maternal preoccupation," but what's in a name?

This orientation to the needs of the baby depends on many things, one of which is that the mother and the father do really carry round with them hidden memories of having been babies themselves, and of having been cared for in terms of reliability, of shielding from unpredictability, and of opportunity to get on with the highly individual matter of personal growth.

So somehow nature has provided for this very acute or even absolute need of babies and small children by making it natural for parents to narrow down their world temporarily, just for a few months, so that the world is there in the middle and not all round outside.

Summary

Stress can be looked at therefore in two ways. One way takes us to a study of the internal stresses and strains inherent in emotional growth. The other way has more practical significance (unless we are psycho-analysts) in that here stress results from relative or gross failure in the environmental provision. These failures can be described in terms of unreliability, destruction of trust, the letting in of unpredictability, and a once and for all or a repeat pattern of the breakup of the continuity of the individual child's line of life.

On the whole those who care for children are found by careful selection, not taught in class.

Babies are quite good at selecting their own mothers, at any rate in respect of this matter of primary maternal preoccupation. Beyond that, I doubt whether I would rate them so highly. But they have to make use of what they find they have as parents.

[1969]

Original Source of Each Chapter

1. "Health Education through Broadcasting," written for *Mother and Child*, No. 28, 1957.
2. "For Stepparents." On January 3, 1955, a talk was given on the BBC's Woman's Hour by a stepmother, telling in a vivid and moving way how she was tormented by being unable to love her stepson, who had joined her household when he was seven years old. The BBC received an enormous number of letters after this broadcast, telling of like and of different experiences in stepparenting and generally indicating that the subject was worth pursuing. As a result the BBC allocated three slots to this end in the Woman's Hour of the following June 6, 7, and 9. The first of these consisted of a series of questions and answers between an expert and a stepfather. The next two were talks given by Winnicott, and are reproduced here. Both were transcribed from tapes, with the result that the punctuation has had to be added.
3. "What Do We Know about Babies as Cloth Suckers?" BBC broadcast talk given January 31, 1956.
4. "Saying 'No'." Three BBC broadcast talks given January 25 and February 1 and 8, 1960.
5. "Jealousy." Four BBC broadcast talks given February 15, 22, and 29 and March 7, 1960.
6. "What Irks?" Three BBC broadcast talks given on March 14, 21, and 28, 1960.

7. "Security." BBC broadcast talk given April 18, 1960. First published under the title "On Security" in *The Family and Individual Development*. London, Tavistock Publications, 1965.
8. "Feeling Guilty." Discussion with Claire Rayner. BBC broadcast talk given March 13, 1961.
9. "The Development of a Child's Sense of Right and Wrong." BBC broadcast talk given June 11, 1962.
10. "Now They Are Five." BBC broadcast talk given June 25, 1962. First published under the title "The Five-Year-Old" in *The Family and Individual Development*. London: Tavistock Publications, 1965.
11. "The Building up of Trust." Written in December, 1969. Never published.

Bibliographical Note

THE WORKS OF D. W. WINNICOTT

Clinical Notes on Disorders of Childhood. 1931. London: William Heinemann Ltd.

The Child and the Family: First Relationships. 1957. London: Tavistock Publications Ltd.

The Child and the Outside World: Studies in Developing Relationships. 1957. London: Tavistock Publications Ltd.

Collected Papers: Through Paediatrics to Psychoanalysis. 1958. London: Tavistock Publications. New York: Basic Books, Inc., Publishers.

The Child, the Family and the Outside World. 1964. London: Penguin Books. Reading, Massachusetts: Addison-Wesley Publishing Co., Inc.

The Maturational Processes and the Facilitating Environment. 1965. London: Hogarth Press and the Institute of Psychoanalysis. New York: International Universities Press.

The Family and Individual Development. 1965. London: Tavistock Publications Ltd.

Playing and Reality. 1971. London: Tavistock Publications Ltd. New York: Basic Books.

Therapeutic Consultations in Child Psychiatry. 1971. London: Hogarth Press and the Institute of Psychoanalysis. New York: Basic Books, Inc., Publishers.

The Piggle: An Account of the Psycho-Analytical Treatment of a Little Girl. 1978. London: Hogarth Press and the Institute of Psychoanalysis. New York: International Universities Press.

Deprivation and Delinquency. 1984. London: Tavistock Publications.

Holding and Interpretation: Fragment of an Analysis. 1986. London: Hogarth Press and the Institute of Psychoanalysis.

Home Is Where We Start From. 1986. London: Penguin Books. New York: W. W. Norton & Company, Inc.

Babies and Their Mothers. 1987. Reading, Massachusetts: Addison-Wesley Publishing Co., Inc.

The Spontaneous Gesture: Selected Letters of D. W. Winnicott. 1987. F. Robert Rodman, Ed. Cambridge, Massachusetts: Harvard University Press.

Human Nature. 1988. New York: Schocken Books.

Psychoanalytic Explorations. 1989. Cambridge, Massachusetts: Harvard University Press.

Talking to Parents. 1993. Reading, Massachusetts: Addison-Wesley Publishing Company.

Index

Adolescents, 91–92
Adopted children, 5
Affection, infant's show of,
    18
Ambivalence, universal prob-
    lem of, 129
Anger
    jealousy and, 54, 64
    timing of expression of, 120
Anxiety
    about going to school, 119
    jealousy and, 54
    toleration of, 108
Arguments, annoyance over,
    72, 79
Attitudes, parental
    jealousy and, 59–60, 61–62
    saying "no" and, 35–36

BBC, 6
Biting, 106–107
Bowlby, John, 130
Breast-feeding, 4, 17, 49, 53,
    75

Broadcasting, health education
    through, 1–6

Cloth-sucking, 15–20
Compulsion, cleaning, 96–97
Confidence, infant's loss of, 19
Conflict(s), 129
    inner, 11
    jealousy and, 54
    self-control and, 93
Controls, children's need vs.
    hate for, 92–93

Depression, mother's, child's
    starting school and, 116,
    117
Development
    emotional, 89
    inherited tendency towards,
    123–124
Disloyalty, child's feeling of,
    for enjoying school,
    119–120

Distractions, 23, 26, 34

Electric shock, avoiding,
    23–24, 31
Emotional development, 89
Empathy, 128
Enclosure
    child's emergence from,
        112–113, 115
    child's inability to get out of,
        117
Environmental provision, 89
    parental knowledge of, 124,
        125
    stress coming from, 129–132,
        133
    study of, 132–133
Envy, jealousy and, 48
Extremes, 73
    perception of world in, 7–8, 9

Fairy godmother, stepmother
    as, 12
Fantasy, 9–10, 100, 101,
    107–108
Fathers, saying "no" by, 39, 85
Fears, 96, 99, 105–106
    guilty, 95, 96
Feeding, 17, 18, 19, 107–108
    jealousy and, 48, 49, 50
Finger-sucking, 18
    See also Cloth-sucking
Five-year-olds, 111–114

adapting to school of,
    114–120
Freedom, 88
Frustrations, 90

Good enough parents, 123
Growth, process of, 124–125
Guilt, sense of, 108, 109
Guilty, feeling, 95–103

Hate
    for baby, 11
    for children, 75–76
    jealousy and, 54
    for mother, 8, 10
"Hot," teaching meaning of
    word, 24–25, 27, 31–32

Imagination, 17, 18
Impulses, protecting children
    from their own, 89–90
Information, seeking, 3–4
Inner psychic reality, 131
Insecurity, defending against,
    90
    See also Security
Instincts, experience of, 107
Integration, 108
Interaction, 126
Internal process, stress coming
    from, 126–129, 133
Interruptions, 84

Irksome matters, 65, 85–86
  discussions of, by mothers,
    65–72, 79–85
  and invasion of mother's
    privacy by children,
    72–79

Jealousy, 41, 81
  abnormal, 62–64
  age of children and, 44, 48,
    51
  beginning of, 47–48
  coming to terms with, 42
  disappearance of, 53–56, 58
  discussions of, by mothers,
    42–50, 56–58, 60, 63–64
  envy and, 48
  love and, 41–42, 54, 58
  between mother and child,
    97–98
  parental attitude and, 59–60,
    61–62
  possession and, 51–53

Knowledge, useful parental,
  124–125

Love
  of baby at birth, absence of,
    in mother, 4, 11
  and jealousy, 41–42, 54, 58
Lovelace, Richard, 88

Matches, playing with, 24
Maternal function, 115
Me and not-me, infant's distinguishing between, 19
Morality
  development of child's,
    105–110
  mother's version of, 38–39
Mothers, discussions by
  of irksome matters, 65–72,
    79–85
  of jealousy, 42–50, 56–58,
    60, 63–64
  of saying "no," 21–26, 31–35
Mothers, privacy, invasion of
  by children, 72–79

Nail-biting, 119
"No," saying, 21
  discussions of, by mothers,
    21–26, 31–35
  by fathers, 39, 85
  stages of, 27–28, 29–30, 31,
    35–39
Nursery school, 113–114

Objects
  adopted by infant, 16, 18–19
  child's addiction to, 118–119
Overprotectiveness, 87

Planning, 82–83

Possession, jealousy and, 51–53
Predictability/unpredictability, 130–132, 133
Pregnancy, 76–77
Primary maternal preoccupation, 133, 134
Privacy, invasion of mother's, by children, 72–79
Prohibition, 37
Psycho-analysis, 127
Psychology, child, instruction in, 5–6

Rayner, Claire, 95–103
Reality principle, introducing, 37
Reflex activities, 17–18
Reliability/unreliability, 130, 131, 132, 133
Resentments, 75, 78
Resilience, 111
Responsibility, parental, 36–37
guilt and, 101–103
Rhythm, adapting to each child's, 81–82
Right and wrong, development of child's sense of, 105–110
Robertson, James and Joyce, "A Two-Year-Old Goes to Hospital," 130

School, child's adapting to, 114–120

Security, children's need for, 87–93
Self-confidence, 88
Self-control, 93
Slapping, 25, 32, 39
Stepparents, 7–13
Stories, bedtime, 80
Stress, 121, 133
coming from environmental provision, 129–132, 133
coming from internal process, 126–129, 133

Teaching, danger of, 123–124
Temper tantrums, 76
Thumb-sucking, 15, 20, 119
See also Cloth-sucking
Tiredness among mothers, causes of, 66, 67
Trauma, persecution theory of, 127–128
Trust, baby's, for mother, 37–38
building up of, 121–134

Unsuccess story, value of, 10–13
Untidiness, mother's task of eternal, 33, 34–35

"Wicked stepmother," myth of, 7–10
Wordsworth, William, 113, 118

D. W. Winnicott

1896–1971

Dr. Winnicott began his medical career in paediatrics and kept an interest in the physiological side of paediatrics while becoming more and more involved in the study of child psychology. His contributions to our understanding of human development, based on extensive clinical work with mothers, babies, and young children, are internationally known and valued.

Dr. Winnicott began his medical studies at Jesus College, Cambridge, and after a period of war service continued them at St. Bartholomew's Hospital in London. Apart from his year as a resident at St. Bartholomew's, his hospital appointments were all at children's hospitals. Dr. Winnicott practised and taught child psychiatry and psycho-analysis for over forty years and was elected president of the British Psycho-Analytical Society. He was a prolific contributor to psycho-analytic and medical journals and lectured widely on child development to many groups of professionals in this field: teachers, midwives, parents, social workers, magistrates, and physicians as well as to psycho-analysts and psychiatrists. Among his best-known books are *Through Paediatrics to Psycho-analysis, The Child, the Family, and the Outside World, The Maturational Processes and the Facilitating Environment,* and *Playing and Reality.*